Developing Scenario-Based Learning

Developing Scenario-Based Learning

Practical insights for tertiary educators

Edited by
Edward Peter Errington

d_p

Dunmore Press

©2003 Edward Peter Errington
©2003 Dunmore Press Ltd

First Published in 2003
by
Dunmore Press Ltd
P.O. Box 5115
Palmerston North
New Zealand
http://www.dunmore.co.nz

Australian Supplier:
Federation Press
P.O. Box 45
Annandale 2038 NSW
Australia
Ph: (02) 9552-2200
Fax: (02) 9552-1681

ISBN 0-86469-443-1

Text:	Minion 11/13
Printer:	The Dunmore Printing Company Ltd
	Palmerston North
Cover design:	Creative Rage, Palmerston North

**This book can be supplied in the UK if ordered by email on
books@dunmore.co.nz**

Contents

Acknowledgements

This book has been made possible thanks to the generous contributions made by colleagues at Massey University, New Zealand, and by guest contributors from the United Kingdom. Common to all is a passion for using scenario-based learning (SBL) to optimise students' conceptual and practical knowledge, and to make assessment strategies more relevant to their chosen profession. At the same time, each contributor offers a unique insight into the application of SBL principles and practices to their own discipline area – with attendant subject content, historically based delivery mode, and respective theory–practice weighting. Each contributor offers valuable insights into the ways they approach SBL with their own cohort of adult learners as would-be professionals in a particular discipline.

I would also like to express my gratitude to Mr Gordon Suddaby, Director of the Training and Development Unit at Massey University, for his unequivocal support for this venture. Thanks also to my wife, Rowena, who gave her time generously as a second reader on many of the chapters.

Edward Peter Errington
March 2003

Introduction

Edward Peter Errington

Welcome to this collection of ideas, practices and reflections on the uses of scenario-based learning (SBL). This is a book for tertiary teachers from all disciplines, as well as staff developers who operate across institutions. It aims to help teachers plan, construct, deliver, evaluate and reflect on the uses of SBL in a systematic way.

I start by outlining why I believe such a book is necessary at this time, and how the collection came into existence by necessity in the search for learning resources. I then outline the reasons why SBL is used. This leads naturally to describing the aims of this specific collection of chapters. I then explain the four-part structure which is in accord with the main areas of scenario-based learning, namely: a skills-based approach; a problem-based approach; an issues-based approach; and a speculative-based approach to SBL. Finally, I summarise the content of the contributory chapters within the context of the four identifiable approaches.

A beginning is made with a brief discussion about the rationale for this book. Why a book on scenario-based learning?

A rationale for a book about scenario-based learning

The idea for a book such as this has been taking shape for some twenty-five years since I first, initially as a primary teacher and later as a secondary drama specialist, involved students in a range of scenarios that they and/or I created with particular learning intentions in mind. I have vivid recollections of their excitement as they explored ideas, tried out new concepts, looked at 'life' from various perspectives and occasionally came away with a sense of wonder at what they had managed to achieve through their involvement. The 'scenarios' usually consisted of a presented set of circumstances, accompanied by the description of a problem, or an issue, or a (communication) skill to be demonstrated, or an invitation to speculate on future/past events. Common to all of these was the element of interaction, either between students, or between individual students and their own study materials. I remember most students as being motivated, thriving on purposeful engagement and growing more capable of reflecting on their learning.

The students, then as now, learn from direct involvement/enactment, or more indirectly by simply imagining and discussing possible actions in reaction to a given (usually written) scenario. The latter are quite popular as examination questions: students are given information and asked to assume particular professional roles, and within this context are required to respond to a given task – their response to the task becomes their answer to the examination question/task.

I remember speculating on the ways that an exploration of real-life events and understandings (enacted, or simply projected in the mind) might be channelled to promote the learning of students from a variety of discipline areas; even working with the same students who at the time were required to digest banks of information and pour this out for examinations. By contrast, a scenario-based approach would contain dramatic qualities – ones that can be used to help students bridge the gap between theory and practice. These dramatic qualities include spontaneous communication, decision-making, assumption of (future) roles and responsibilities, replication of human processes and procedures, and the simulation of real-world settings to explore past, present and future scenarios.

We all possess what Courtney (1980) labels 'dramatic imagination'. We naturally project our thoughts and feelings, our inner dramas about the past (what was/might have been), present (what is), and future (what might be), to guide our actions (or inactivity). Each lived or imagined scenario contains significant people, problems/ challenges, considered actions/choices, and projected/experienced outcomes. Our ability to envision the future, make sense of the past and cope with the present is fundamental to all our human activities.

Now, some decades later, with rich experiences as a teacher educator, staff developer and training consultant, I am pleased to observe a growing confidence in the uses of scenario-based learning. In my current position I have a remit to help academic staff optimise student learning and increase their repertoire of teaching strategies. I am in a fortunate position to observe and appreciate, and occasionally deliver, scenario-based learning (SBL) across discipline areas.

Notably, more and more tertiary teachers are moving away from a traditional, fact-only approach to teaching towards one that helps students (as would-be professionals) create bridges between theory and informed professional practice. Contributors to this collection of scenario-based learning examples come either from Massey University, where there is a high incidence of SBL usage, or from parts of the United Kingdom where SBL is undergoing a renaissance – thanks to advocates of problem-based learning who employ scenarios to achieve learning purposes.

The overarching term 'scenario-based learning' (SBL), as used in this edited collection, refers to any educational approach that involves the use of, or is dependent on, scenarios to bring about desired learning intentions. Scenarios may constitute a set of circumstances, a description of human behaviour, an outline of events, a story of human endeavour, an incident within a professional setting, a human dilemma/problem/issue and/or any other means that focuses on the interactions of humans with each other and their world. The common denominator is the notion of using scenarios for educational purposes. When we are asked to meet a growing demand for SBL resources to support initiatives, it becomes clear to us through various hard copy/electronic literature searches that SBL assumes a plethora of different names. In various contexts it is referred to as goal-based learning, critical incidents, enigmas, role-play (specific kinds), triggers, or simulation (involving scenarios), among others. These names also refer to different kinds of scenario usage. The joint realisation that SBL is important for all learners and that there is a confusing literature in this area prompted the creation of this edited work.

Yes, but why use scenario-based learning?

It was discovered that contributors mainly used scenarios for students to:

- demonstrate professional skills, abilities, and theoretical principles as a result of participating in scenarios that require replication of tasks normally found within a particular (chosen) professional setting (**Skills-based scenarios**)

- experience problem-solving and problem-seeking processes, drawing upon (realistic) examples similar to those found in 'real' professional settings (**Problem-based scenarios**)

- explore a range of issues that impact on important decision-making processes, and other professional judgements that have to be made/considered as part of the work of professionals in the workplace (**Issues-based scenarios**).

- speculate on, then empathise with, the thoughts and feelings of the human agents within the professional setting. First, this involves students experiencing the scenario, and then reflecting on their feelings as a consequence of this experience. Second, it challenges students to examine the emotional states of other social actors within the same scenario to promote empathy with their (subsequent) clients, families of clients, and professional colleagues. The element of speculation arises as students 'guess' and come to understand the real emotional states of 'significant others' encountered in professional settings (**Speculative-based scenarios**).

Aims of the book

In light of the above, the overall intention of this book is to provide teachers, teacher educators, and staff developers alike with insights and practical strategies for using scenarios to optimise students' learning opportunities.

Each of the fourteen contributors provides working examples of successful, 'warts and all', scenario-based vignettes. To render a sense of cohesiveness across chapters, each contributor was asked to address five fundamental questions:

- Why employ SBL with your students? (**Learning intentions**)
- Where does this learning take place? (**Learning context**)

- How do you put SBL into practice? (**Practical strategies**)
- What do you **make of** your practices? (**Reflection on practice**)
- What advice can you give those teachers wishing to adopt similar approaches themselves? (**Lessons learned**)

How is the book organised and what does it contain?

This book is divided into four parts that deal with skills-based, problem-based, issues-based and speculative-based scenarios. Each one includes details of the individual SBL approach 'in a nutshell'. It encompasses learning purposes, the kinds of knowledge construction students are expected to engage in, and a brief description of the chapters in this book that exemplify the approach.

PART ONE: Skills-based scenarios offers examples of scenario-based learning that are used to develop, and/or help students demonstrate acquired professional skills. In this orientation participants are required to acquire a skill, ability or set of professional attitudes; these are often modelled via demonstrated behaviour based on set criteria. Students may be asked to rehearse this attribute or professional stance until it is fully internalised, using the criteria as a guide for appropriate professional behaviour. The main purpose of this approach is to help students demonstrate acquired knowledge, or specific professional skills or abilities.

The following are our examples:

In Chapter 1, Susan Brock shares her informed views and practical ideas to guide readers through the construction of scenarios for specific learning purposes. She uses a process with the acronym 'PIA PRISM' alongside a reflective cycle of planning, presenting and evaluating SBL to provide a useful 'scaffold' on which we can support our own scenario initiatives. She explains some of the intricacies of scenario creation – ones she hopes readers will appreciate and then apply with understanding to their own creations. This is an ideal opening practical chapter.

In Chapter 2, Sandra Gammer focuses on the use(s) of scenarios designed so that students can achieve a range of theoretical understandings and practical skills within clinical settings. In particular, her students get involved in the presented scenario, are required to respond to a number of focal questions to guide their attention and are then asked to reflect on their experience. This is a popular process used by teachers who employ scenario-based learning to help students acquire specific professional skills.

In Chapter 3, Kim van Wissen reveals how she employs a number of different scenarios to help her students critically appraise some taken-for-granted rituals and routines embedded within some professional settings. The promotion of (critical) reflective practice skills is an essential ingredient of most, if not all, areas of professional education. Scenarios provide the right impetus for asking questions of roles, responsibilities and the professional contexts where these are negotiated.

In **Chapter 4, Stephen Bell and Rachel Page** take us through a series of practical steps involved in creating a scenario-based-learning (computer) package designed to promote their students' decision-making skills. They explain the learning intentions, the choice of scenario, the developmental process for decision-making and the integration of this and other concepts into a valuable set of study resources – ones that can be used to develop a useful interactive computer package for facilitating skills-based approaches to SBL.

Skills-based approaches are useful in learning situations where the knowledge to be acquired appears 'fixed', has clearly defined steps or procedures and focuses on practical rather than theoretical expression, and where professional roles and attendant responsibilities are made clear. The scenarios are clearly defined, with set tasks.

PART TWO: Problem-based scenarios centres on the use of SBL to engage students in processes of problem solving and problem seeking. A problem-based approach involves students *investigating* specific information in order to arrive at conclusions that have not been predetermined. In a problem-orientation, participants are required to draw on their knowledge of the discipline area; use their own appropriate working knowledge; apply this knowledge to a series of challenges; react appropriately to problems as they arise; and arrive at considered solutions based on justified reasons. One main purpose of this approach is to have students apply knowledge to the solution of problems.

Here are our examples:

In **Chapter 5, Tim Parkinson** describes, analyses and evaluates his problem-based approach to SBL. He takes a real field setting to constitute a whole, 'real-world' scenario which encompasses a series of complex processes. He then helps students assume a 'concrete' diagnostic approach to solving the emergent problem. In so doing, he places greater value on the learning process than on any particular set of solutions students might arrive at and subsequently have to justify.

In **Chapter 6, Errol Thompson** relates how he managed to construct a scenario that provided the focal point for a whole paper/course. He discusses the journey made (in common with other teachers now using SBL) from relying on traditional-only approaches to learning delivery to using approaches that engages students in problem-solving at all levels. He shows how one overarching scenario can be used to facilitate an open-ended problem environment for teaching, learning and assessment.

In **Chapter 7, Terry Stewart** reminds us that life itself is full of personal and professional challenges and that problems face us everywhere we care to look. As a consequence, we experience problem-based living. He sees that the challenge is to optimise the use of problem-solving skills in the classroom. He shares with us how he engages students in a range of 'reality-based' scenarios, getting them to solve various problems and meet different learning challenges. This process incorporates the use of computer-based simulation. In this virtual scenario they are able to interrogate, explore, make mistakes and learn from their experiences.

In Chapter 8, Moira McLoughlin, Christine Hogg and Angela Darvill, identify significant issues surrounding the development and practical implementation of a study module that uses a problem-based scenario to raise the cultural awareness of students as would-be professionals. While relating this approach, they discuss aspects of scenario construction such as: the relevance of the amount of student interest; the notion of a meaningful context; the students' prior learning; the acquisition of 'new' knowledge; and the role of the teacher/tutor.

In Chapter 9, Eula Miller, Sophie Smailes, Sheila Stark, Clare Street and Katherine Watson describe and evaluate their uses of a problem-based approach to SBL designed to help capture the complex, multi-layered nature of professional settings. Using scenarios taken from real life events they show us how students are guided to explore issues of 'diversity' (stereotypes, group norms, personal values), to reflect on the 'messiness' of living in a social and culturally diverse society, and to consider their own impact on these contexts and how these gained insights might be applied to their chosen professional setting. Each scenario offers a problem that demands exploration and the recognition of alternative solutions.

Problem-based approaches to SBL are useful where there is a desire to explore processes of decision-making and where students are required to apply their knowledge in demanding circumstances; be spontaneous in response to changing circumstances; have a fundamental grasp of basic human organisations; explore issues and events at a very deep level over a lengthy period of time; and gain from exploring notions of 'consensus' and 'difference' as part of human dynamics.

PART THREE: Issues-based scenarios focuses on the use of scenarios to promote students' understanding about a range of issues. Having researched an issue, students assume and then defend an informed position in response to the issue-laden scenario. Students actively explore an issue by assuming the positions of the real-life human agents and then contend with each other to bring about desired outcomes. They usually reveal the ways by which stands on issues are informed and contested, based on vested interests.

In an issues-based approach, participants are required to investigate the attitudes, beliefs and values surrounding an issue; investigate the attitudes, beliefs and values held by the relevant human agencies; take a particular stand on an issue; enter into a scenario where this stand is revealed, articulated, possibly defended and evaluated in relation to similar or dissimilar positions represented by other students; align themselves with role-players holding similar positions; negotiate or contend with those holding dissimilar positions; and, possibly, take an opposing stand on an issue. A main aim of this approach is to enable students to compare and contrast positions taken on issues.

Here are our examples:

In Chapter 10, Judith Bernanke recounts her experiences of using student-centred scenarios to explore a range of issues underpinning 'cultural sensitivity' – with a particular focus on 'ethnocentrism'. She critically evaluates the benefits and associated risks of using issues-based scenarios to enhance cultural sensitivity – particularly if the selected scenarios depend heavily on the uses of role-play for their construction and delivery.

In Chapter 11, Juliana Mansvelt reveals how she uses an issue-based SBL approach to promote students' active engagement with theoretical material presented in the rest of her paper/course. She also uses this approach as a vehicle for students to consider the assumptions they bring to the scenario decisions: ones that are bound in space, time, and their own understanding of 'Where in the world am I?' In common with other contributors, she sees the process of issue exploration as more important to the learning process than is the arrival at any one solution.

In Chapter 12, Edward Errington focuses on the use of scenario-based learning to involve students directly by having them investigate their own positions on gender issues. He shows how student-constructed scenarios can offer different perspectives: that of the creator, those of the various social actors within the scenario and those of different members of the audience observing the unfolding events. During an analysis of these multiple perspectives, he discusses the efficacy of this issues-based approach for achieving desired learning intentions.

Issues-based approaches are useful in learning situations where not all the facts are known (there is an element of uncertainty/a need for further or continuing research); where the selected issue requires genuine investigation (outcomes are not known in advance); where the selected issue lends itself to a variety of comparative perspectives; and where positions on an issue require both evaluation and justification.

Part Four: Speculative-based scenarios explores the uses of SBL where students speculate on experiences, observations, or given information. The focus is on questions such as: 'What would happen if…?' , 'What might have happened?' or 'How might such and such a person feel, in the light of this or that information?' Students are required to speculate upon and justify their choices. In a speculative-based approach participants are required to generate knowledge to fill in gaps between known and unknown information; use 'evidence' to make informed judgements; and reconstruct and then represent particular human interactions. This approach to SBL is used to:

- have students speculate on uncertainties surrounding held beliefs and knowledge
- facilitate legitimate expression for students' own/others' attitudes and feelings
- develop empathetic understanding.

The following are our examples:

In Chapter 13, Regina Pernice outlines the uses of 'writing-in-role' when incorporated within/alongside the scenario. She explains how this experience helps students explore the emotional dimensions within professional settings. Students have an opportunity to record their thoughts and feelings from the standpoint of each human actor within the given, realistic scenario. The aim is to develop an understanding of and empathy with the nature and experience of mental illness as it impacts on the patient, the patient's family and the broader community. The ability of would-be practitioners to empathise with the relevant human actors is an essential feature of sound professional development. 'Speculation' features to the extent that students are required to project themselves into 'someone else's shoes' and from there create a reality and develop understanding and an empathetic response. They are being asked to write-in-role, in response to questions such as: 'How would/do you think/feel when in this person's position?' and 'What do you write in this context'?

In Chapter 14, Mary Murray presents a case study of SBL focusing on death, dying, mortality and immortality. She asks students to imagine they live at some point in the future when scientists have found a way of enabling humans to live forever. There follows a rigorous examination of this 'What if?' question as students work through the personal and social implications of emergent possibilities. The overall aim of this exploration is for students to reflect on their own lives so that they can achieve a richer, fuller life.

Speculative-based approaches are useful for learning situations where students have sufficient information about the past, present or future scenario upon which to make their speculative predictions and where:

- they must fill in the gaps between known and unknown information
- they need to reach and justify informed conclusions
- they require practice at making reasoning processes explicit and have to use evidence or artefacts in a systematic way
- the ability to predict or explain human phenomena is valued.

Now you are more fully aware of each particular approach to scenario-based learning, the contributors to this collection hope that you will gain from knowing more about how each is created, delivered, evaluated, reflected on, and learned from.

References

Courtney, R., 'Our dramatic universe', in R. Courtney, *The Dramatic Curriculum*, Drama Book Specialists, London, Ontario, 1980.

Part One

Skills-based Scenarios

1

Creating scenarios using a reflective cycle and 'PIA PRISM'

Susan Brock

Introduction

When I first started using problem-based learning (PBL) at Wolverhampton I had an understanding of what it was and how it compared with other approaches to teaching and learning. However, I did not have a sense of how I could write effective and interesting scenarios. Consideration of the literature revealed some interesting ideas, which will be discussed later, but I did not have a sense of how I could incorporate them into my practice. I wanted to know:

- What makes a "good" scenario?
- How can I learn how to write one, what tools can I use?
- How will I know if the scenario was effective, can I evaluate it?
- Is there a way of providing feedback to ensure I learn too?

This chapter presents the current state of my learning from both theory and practice. In short, I found there were no easy answers and that what I needed to do was learn how to build a base of skills, partly by learning how to ask other questions. Thus, in this chapter I suggest using a reflective cycle to systematically ensure I can reveal a range of issues and factors. Integral to this is a tool, PIA PRISM, which incorporates my sense of the best ideas on scenario writing from the literature. Thus, by the end of the chapter I hope you'll have some good ideas for ways in which you can develop a wide range of skills useful for your practice with SBL.

I have always been keen to see my practice as a teacher as cyclical – I gain awareness of the context within which I am working, I think, read, plan, write and deliver. I then evaluate, rethink, rewrite and so on. Within these processes, I aim to use as many resources as possible to facilitate the growth of my students and myself. In more traditional approaches to teaching and learning, for example, the lecture-based course, it seems reasonably straightforward to make judgements about the efficacy of my lecturing style and myself. I can make my lectures interesting by use of changes in pace, visual aids, handouts etc. I can speak clearly and repeat several times in different ways the points I want students to learn. These are the ways in which I can deliver a "good" lecture and the ways in which I can ask my students to make judgements about my practice.

SBL is, of course, one interesting way of teaching and learning in which these "taken–for-granteds" disappear. It seemed as if I was being asked to write half a page (or so) of interesting text which would then serve as a springboard for a whole host of content-based and process-based learning by students. My role was then to facilitate their group process and their learning directions. But where to start with writing the scenarios? As a consequence, this and my earlier set of questions became the central focus of my deliberations. The literature in an area provides the answers to many of our questions, and sure enough I was pleased to find within the PBL/SBL literature the notion of a problem-based learning "development cycle" (Drummond-Young and Mohide, 2001). This cycle served to ground my thinking around SBL because it is systematic and iterative; I have revised it into a reflective cycle (see Figure 1.1). It contains reference to use of PIA PRISM and this will be explained in some depth. For now, you just need to know that it facilitates stages of the cycle and will therefore also facilitate key aspects of your skills development.

Working around the reflective cycle

If we begin by looking at Figure 1.1, we can see that boxes 2 and 3 of the reflective cycle involve collecting a wide range of different types of information. Obviously, when teachers commence writing course materials, they have a detailed sense of the context they are writing within. Major components of this are the course philosophy, objectives, outcomes and themes. I am not presently involved in planning for a whole course: I now work closely with a team of staff to plan input for the second term in a nine-term nursing course. We have three modules and a practice document to integrate in our term. Our main priorities are to help students understand the social context within which health care is delivered, gain some basic nursing skills and appreciate the different types of evidence available which they may use to underpin their practice.

Other important aspects of the context within which I am currently working are the continuing increase in numbers of students in nurse education in the United Kingdom; widening Higher Education entry gates and entry criteria and working without a full complement of staff, on a campus which barely meets our rooming requirements. We are also due to move to another campus within the next 12 months. My particular module currently runs on two courses (Registered Nurse/Diploma in Higher Education and also the Registered Nurse/Bachelor of Science degree programme). This module is delivered on four different campuses and is taken by a total of nine groups of students, totalling around 700 students, each year. There is a team of around 15 members of staff who work with the students on the different sites.

Figure 1.1 PBL/SBL Reflective Cycle

Box 1	Box 2	Box 3	Box 4
Start, and then continue from here:	Identify the course or programme objectives, outcomes, themes and concepts.	Identify the priority problems and issues for this stage of the course.	Select one or more of these issues or themes and use PIA PRISM's Preparatory Questions **(Fig 1.2)** to generate various mind maps. (Keep these maps for later use.)
Reflect on the process and your perceptions of it. Re-draft and revise materials as appropriate in preparation for future groups. **Box 9**	**Your knowledge of your, and your students', psychological, physical, educational, cultural and intellectual needs, constraints, opportunities and skills.**		Prioritise options based upon your awareness of both your personal and course philosophies. **Box 5**
Use the PIA PRISM Evaluation Form **(Fig 1.3)** to evaluate use of the scenarios, with students and staff. Collate feedback and consider this alongside your original intentions and mind maps. **Box 8**	Work with your students to deliver your scenarios, which will hopefully fit the purpose, be the right length and type, and facilitate integration. They will also be appropriately authentic, relevant and adequately resourced. They should also have impact, generate interest and use different modalities. **Box 7**		Develop the supplementary materials, such as: a Resources Handbook, facilitator guides, timetables, fixed resource sessions etc. **Box 6**

So, having drawn together the above documents, we then use the Preparatory Questions sheet from PIA PRISM (Figure 1.2) in order to actually start to write the scenarios which will facilitate learning. I'd suggest that these activities have two main stages (see boxes 4 and 5 in Figure 1.1). When using the preparatory questions, I have found that we produce many ideas in the form of answers grounded in our sense of our practice and the course we are working on. This stage (box 4) is really quite good fun and may most usefully be conducted in an informal way with lots of flip-chart paper. This is preferable to using a whiteboard (I have personally wiped off material I later wished I'd kept).

Some of the questions I have included at this stage are concerned with the philosophy of what I am trying to do when using SBL, and others are about practicalities. For example, I may assume that experienced SBL learners can work through a complex scenario without using any fixed resources (such as a lecture or video or printed materials), whereas students with little confidence may experience less initial anxiety if their transition to more independent learning is facilitated by the provision of a variety of fixed resource materials. At this stage (box 5) we make overt and transparent all the assumptions inherent at the different levels of our course and our individual philosophies.

The next stage of the reflective cycle is important because this is the first opportunity I have to determine if our ideas will "fit" with the day-to-day running of the course. It is when we work out if we will have enough lecture theatres available for the fixed resource sessions and if we have enough small classrooms available for the small group work. I may write a 20-page SBL handbook for use with several hundred students, and must decide whether it would be more efficient to locate it on a website or to get it printed out. I also need to think through which staff will be likely to wish to facilitate these particular students and what their preferences may be. For example, some staff feel more comfortable with facilitators' notes to guide them around the content of scenarios, while others feel confident with the SBL process and are able to allow students to work with the content they consider is important.

So, when I have finished planning what size the groups will be, how many scenarios they will work through, in what time period, with which resources available to them, I am then ready to work with the facilitators. I help them decide what resources they will require to support the students on their campus and assist them to provide these. We should then be ready to work with the students (box 7). If I've answered all the PIA PRISM preparatory questions with a reasonable degree of knowledge and insight, the students should enjoy working though interesting scenarios which stimulate them to know more about a variety of issues, topics etc. They should be motivated, and should be able to identify and access a range of materials that help them to meet the learning outcomes they have set themselves.

However, where student learning is concerned, I never find it particularly helpful to rely on what "should" occur. Obviously, we have many different methods of determining the success of teaching and learning but I like to supplement these with an evaluation form (box 8). I am particularly concerned with staff and students' perceptions of their experience. For example, the scenario should, or could, have motivated them to learn, but did it? I can determine this from students' inclusions in both summative and formative assessments but also from the PIA PRISM Evaluation Form. I have shown the questions from this form in Figure 1.3. The material they choose to include and how they use it in assignments tell me something about the level the students are at when they undertake the assessment tasks. However, their materials and method tell me little about the utility of the scenario in facilitating the acquisition of skills and knowledge – not least because I don't always have a definite sense of exactly what the learning process has "added" for every student.

I use polarised (yes or no) responses on the actual Evaluation Form. Some of my colleagues have criticized this method for obvious reasons. However, as I have to collate responses from some 700 forms every year, I selected the simple yes or no response because of its ease of use. You could, of course, develop this further to suit your particular "need to know". I also group into themes the more qualitative responses provided on the bottom of the form and include quotations from this in information I produce for future groups of students.

At this point I go on to compare both staff and students' feedback on the scenario with our original intentions. I'm always intrigued to determine if our hopes and ideas have been realised – and what serendipitous gains have been made, too! This stage of the reflective cycle is particularly important – where I compare what we intended with what we feel happened and then gain a sense of possible directions for the future. Note that the PIA PRISM evaluation form is simply that: a communication tool available for use by all participants in your SBL/PBL. I publish the collated feedback to both staff and students and indicate possible future changes to them too.

In completing the cycle, much depends upon the time period that elapses between iterations of your course. I find it useful to complete the reflection, redrafting and revision stage (box 9) as soon as possible. I jot down my impressions and ideas straight away and then subsequently return to the reflective cycle at Stage 1, shortly before commencing work with the next group. Thus, using the cycle and PIA PRISM as suggested above, I can follow how I grow and develop alongside my students. For me, these changes take place in many ways. I have a transparent record of my intentions and evidence of the SBL participant's perspectives on how these were perceived and received. I also have a sense of how "good" the scenario may have been, because integral to PIA PRISM are various notions (from the literature, to be discussed below) of what is required for a scenario to be effective. I take mostly "yes" responses, most of the time, as indicating a scenario that really did facilitate learning.

However, do beware. Use of the reflective cycle and PIA PRISM together reveal some interesting conundrums. For example, one particular scenario was evaluated by some students as "motivating", but they felt that they had neither sufficient time nor resources available to help them meet their outcomes. As a group of staff we had quite a lot of debate about this. If students were motivated to learn, but did not learn all they wanted to, did this say more about their aspirations, the resources available, their skills and knowledge base or what? So, I'd advise use of the tools offered in this chapter as simply one way in which you can develop the skills you'll find helpful to work with such complex phenomena. I do not pretend to have found all the answers!

PIA PRISM – preparatory questions and evaluation form

Now you have had some chance to become familiar with the reflective cycle, I'll work through the two main parts of PIA PRISM (the preparatory questions and the evaluation form) in a little more depth. The acronym PIA PRISM represents: Purpose, Integration, Authenticity, Prevalence and relevance, Resources and format, Impact and interest, Sequentialism and complexity, and finally Modality. I chose an acronym to pull these aspects together, primarily because I find them helpful. These ideas are presented visually in Figure 1.4. The precise nature of these individual components will be explained presently.

Figure 1.2 PIA PRISM – Preparatory Questions

PIA PRISM

Preparatory questions: to ask yourselves when writing your scenario

Purpose

Why are you writing the scenario? What are the possible learning outcomes?

Do you want to ensure students cover a specific area of material/knowledge?

Will students develop knowledge of concepts, ideas, theories or techniques?

Is the focus of the SBL activity to be the knowledge of content that students have already acquired; or the skills they will acquire as a consequence of engaging with the process, or a mixture of both?

Integration

Which subjects do you want the students to integrate knowledge from? How will you indicate which subjects areas they may need to work within? For example, could you include laboratory reports, a drug card, or X-rays?

Authenticity

How 'authentic' or 'pure' do you want the SBL activity to be? Will you give your facilitators any content-based direction? Will your facilitators give any content-based direction to students?

Prevalence and relevance

Do you want yours to revolve around a common clinical scenario? Or do you want to include one for its unique value? How will you ensure students will find it relevant to their understanding of the world?

Resources and format for delivery

What material resources will be available to students? What will you recommend and how? What will be the balance between the resources you supply or prescribe and the resources they will source themselves? How many hours will you, and they, devote to SBL? What will be the balance of facilitated hours in the classroom/group and hours spent individually sourcing materials? What skills and knowledge base may students currently have to build on? How will you ensure the scenario is just far enough outside their current levels to stretch them in an enjoyable way? Will your scenarios be delivered electronically or in some other form? How easily can you produce, distribute and use the medium you have chosen?

cont'd ...

Impact and interest

What do you know about your students' concerns? How will you make sure the scenario is sufficiently interesting to be motivating? Would it be more beneficial to focus on an area in which there is consensus and hard empirical evidence, or on one in which students will appreciate a more relativist ethical position, or a mixture of both? Will you choose a very controversial and/or emotive issue? Do you need to consider provision of 'back-up' resources if the scenario is likely to be very provocative, such as one concerning domestic violence or other abuse?

Sequence, brevity and complexity

Will your scenario consist of a one-line statement, a one-paragraph vignette, a full case history or a whole primary research article? Will the scenario be presented in 'parts', sequentially, over a period of time; for example, following the development of a plan of care? What level of complexity will you weave through the scenario? Will you make it very difficult to untangle or will you provide obvious clues?

Modality

Which modality (visual, auditory, kinaesthetic or a mixture of them all) will you use to stimulate the students? Could you use film, a taped episode, a picture, or a role-play? Do you want to reach students on a deeper personal level or do you want to try to separate this from the professional?

In general, the individual components of PIA PRISM arose due to my sense of the most useful ideas in the PBL/SBL literature on scenario writing. For example, Delisles (1997) was particularly influential, because he provides a simple checklist that served as the inspiration for the PIA PRISM evaluation form. He indicates the use of this at the scenario writing stage, but its simple questions and polarised, convergent responses are probably more helpful during the evaluation of the scenario. Nevertheless, he argues strongly and convincingly that problem-based scenarios should be based on student experience, be developmental, and be curriculum-based. In addition, Dewey (1916:157) suggests that problems should be "large enough to challenge" and small enough to have "luminous familiar" and novel elements.

Drummond-Young and Mohide (2001:168) suggest the use of seven principles of "effective problem design", the content of which has been fully integrated within PIA PRISM. However, the notion of principles was replaced with use of less prescriptive questions. Nevertheless, it is still not easy to know what to publish for students' use. Hafler (1991: 154), for example, quotes a colleague of hers who was "trying to decide what to pack into this case and what to leave out". Her work is particularly worth reading because it contains many other rich details of her own and her colleagues' problem-writing experiences.

Other work is less obviously useful. For example, Bridges and Hallinger (1998:9) suggest that "programme designers need to devote considerable time and effort" to problem design, and then themselves (unfortunately) devote only 19 lines to it. However, despite its brevity, their work does contain insight, and my sense of this has been

Figure 1.3 Summary of questions taken from the evaluation form

1. Was it clear why this scenario was chosen?
2. Did it help students to meet the learning outcomes for the term/semester?
3. Did students gain content-based knowledge?
4. Did they acquire skills as a consequence of studying the scenario?
5. Did the scenario facilitate students to integrate knowledge and ideas from different subjects?
6. Were you satisfied with the guidance you received in order to work with this scenario?
7. Was the basic subject of the scenario relevant to your 'practice'?
8. Would it have been better to focus on a more general area/issue?
9. Was the scenario easy to use?
10. Was it easily communicated to students?
11. Were sufficient resources available to students?
12. Were sufficient hours allocated to the study of the scenario?
13. Was the right balance of group/individual hours provided?
14. Could these have been allocated more effectively?
15. Did the scenarios have a sufficient knowledge base to enable participants to engage with the scenario?
16. Was the work on the scenario enjoyable?
17. Did the scenario appear to have an impact on students?
18. Did students consider they had learned a lot from this scenario?
19. Did students seem to manage the contradictions and debates in the literature they used?
20. Was the scenario motivating?
21. Was the length of the scenario about right?
22. Should it have been shorter?
23. Was the amount of detail about right?
24. Was the degree of openness (of interpretation) contained within the scenario appropriate?
25. Did the scenario make use of different physical senses, i.e. hearing, seeing, feeling?
26. Did it appear to engage students in a number of different ways?

What is the most important thing you'd like to tell us about the scenario?

What advice would you give to the group of students who will use the scenario next?

Please continue below if you'd like to tell us something in more detail, or if you'd like to comment on something we have not asked about above.

incorporated into PIA PRISM. In other places where you may expect to find insight, it is mysteriously absent, such as in otherwise helpful 'practical' work (i.e. Gibbon, 2000).

Overall, PIA PRISM can be simple to use – two sets of questions to answer – but I find the questions can provoke complex answers. The consequence of the ways in which you ask the questions, and the imagination you use when answering them, should be an appropriate, interesting, motivating scenario. The different sections of PIA PRISM will now be briefly unpacked.

The constituents of PIA PRISM

Purpose

The first sets of questions, around purpose, are perhaps the most fundamental. These encourage me to explore factors which I find we may often take for granted as a team. Exactly what are we trying to do with SBL and the scenario? I find that if I state my intentions at this early stage it helps to keep me focused.

Integration

The questions surrounding integration are really helpful if you are familiar with running a traditional curriculum with traditional subject divisions. It is these questions, which encourage exploration of exactly what subjects and levels and types of material may be integrated by students during use of these particular scenarios. In our second term (mentioned earlier) we remind ourselves we want students to draw insights and knowledge from traditional subject areas such as research, health promotion, sociology and social policy.

Authenticity

The issues surrounding authenticity are particularly important if different members of your team have varying levels of confidence in themselves, the students and the SBL process. There are many hybrid versions of SBL and this, combined with the positions of individual staff, must be debated. We had an important debate about facilitators' notes. Key staff argued that facilitators should be given "content outlines" (with the scenario) that they should then help their students to cover. Other staff argued that students must determine the areas important to them to cover, based upon their priorities and interests. In many ways, it is the answers to authenticity questions that prompt you to revisit your answers to questions about purpose and integration. The time we spent in thought and debate was very useful and vital to our development as a team of staff.

Prevalence and relevance

Prevalence and relevance encourage us to think through what we know about our students and their concerns and also what we know about the links between their experience of the world and our knowledge base. For example, we may wish them to look at a common

Figure 1.4 PIA PRISM represented visually

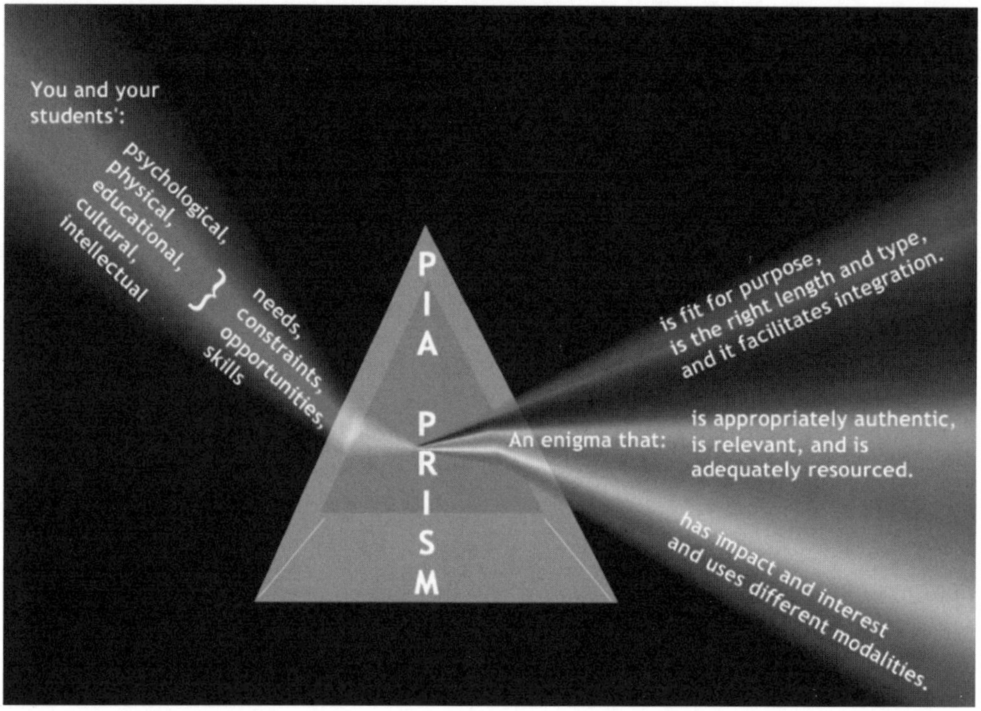

You and your students':

psychological, physical, educational, cultural, intellectual } needs, constraints, opportunities, skills

P
I
A

P
R
I
S
M

An enigma that:

is fit for purpose, is the right length and type, and it facilitates integration.

is appropriately authentic, is relevant, and is adequately resourced.

has impact and interest and uses different modalities.

(This graphic is the work of Nicola Kirby, Courseware Development Unit, School of Health, University of Wolverhampton, UK.)

issue or problem like "social isolation", infection control or coronary heart disease at a basic level, or, they may need to learn about more rare/specialist knowledge and phenomena such as agoraphobia, the role of nurses' scissors in the transmission of MRSA, or heart rates and rhythm such as ventricular tachycardia. We use our judgement about which type of scenario students will learn most from: unique situations, or a more general area because it impacts on many thousands of people on a daily basis.

Resources and format for delivery

Resources and format for delivery are about practicalities, the material realities within learning environments. For example, it may be neither possible nor desirable to photocopy a 20-page article for 300 students or attempt to use a website as the basis for a scenario if the same number of students have only five PCs between them. Likewise, other pragmatic realities of just how many "teacher hours" and how many rooms you have available must be factored in. Even first-level students may not need much facilitation time if they are working on an interesting scenario where sources of information are freely available. I have found it vital to consider how I will provide access to the scenario for both staff and students. For example, I wanted to use the song "So strong" by the artist Labi Sifre as a scenario. If this particular artist had not been prepared to waive copyright on his work, I would have been unable to copy it for distribution to my colleagues. Despite having permission to copy the music I then had to find a way of ensuring 20 members of staff had access to tape recorders to play the music in the classroom.

Impact and interest

Impact and interest are clearly related to relevance, but even the most relevant scenario can be unstimulating if not presented in a way that captures the imagination of students. It is at this point where you may also consider what 'flags' or 'key words' to write into the scenario to suggest to students the type of literature they may find most pertinent. Perhaps even more importantly, you may find that a scenario that has genuine academic interest for one staff member takes on levels of personal interest and connection with other staff and students. It is wise to have contingency plans for supporting students when their interest takes them into areas that previously have been addressed only rarely. I have been intrigued to find that approximately half our nursing students find the song by Labi Sifre more interesting and motivating than scenarios which are more obviously 'nursing' in focus (for example, 'An elderly client, Mary, experiences a needle stick injury as a consequence of the practice of a colleague …').

Sequence, brevity and complexity

Connected to impact and interest are the issues surrounding whether you allow 'the story/scenario to unfold' sequentially or hit students briefly and dramatically with the main thrust of a set of debates or circumstances. It is interesting how we may write something sequential, which we imagine may allow for gradual exposure, and yet students, 'hooked' by the nature of the first parts of a scenario, will quickly take themselves deep into sophisticated and complex literature. As mentioned earlier, your knowledge of your students is vital. You need to know enough about them to have a strong sense of what they may know. This will help you to write the clues or flags which you would use to ensure they consider the material required on, for example, a professional course. Scenarios presented sequentially also seem to lead inexperienced students to "wait for the next bit". Thus, they sometimes hold back, unsure which way you may seem to want them to go next. Scenarios that appear complex to some staff are often quickly reduced by students into areas important to them. As long as they are not scared by jargon, students often surprise me with the learning tasks they are prepared to set themselves.

Modality

Finally, modality is essential to consider. We are all different and operate best on different modalities. Just as good teachers will provide material easily accessible by people who are auditory, visual or kinaesthetic, facilitators who wish to engage the maximum number of students will ensure they think about whether to present students with film clips, audio tape, music, print media and so on. Photographs seem to be particularly useful and the Labi Sifre song mentioned earlier always intrigues students, who quickly and readily disentangle the lyrics.

Having worked through the preparatory questions in PIA PRISM (Figure 1.2), if you now turn to the summary of questions taken from the evaluation form (Figure 1.3), you will notice how scenario users are asked questions which help reveal the extent to which they believed the scenario achieved what they intended. This summary can also provide you with the questions, and subsequent responses, you require to complete the final part of your reflective cycle. Both the cycle and PIA PRISM contain my sense of the best of the current ideas available at the time of writing. I have packaged them in a way which I hope you'll find both accessible and versatile.

Conclusion

In conclusion, this chapter has presented details of my journey into writing scenarios and summarises where I am at present in my learning. I feel the "tools" I have written have helped develop my scenario-writing skills in many ways. My practice is more focused, I have become more student-led, I have a deeper understanding of the educational aims of SBL, I am more reflective, I find it easier to collaborate with colleagues and I know how my students respond to my approach to my teaching and learning practice on several levels. I consider these changes are taking place primarily because I am constantly prepared to ask the types of questions contained in PIA PRISM. I think I have become the Socratic wise (wo)man – I know what it is I do not know, and I value the process of different ways of "finding out". In short, I hope I model the type of learner SBL will facilitate my students to become. In the process, of course, I also further refine my skills and abilities surrounding scenario writing.

References

Bridges, E. and Hallinger, P. (1998), 'Problem-based learning in medical and managerial education', in Fogarty, R. (1998), *Problem-based learning,* Arlington Heights: Skylight professional development.

Delisle, R. (1997), *How to use problem-based learning in the classroom,* Virginia: ASCD.

Dewey, J. (1916), *Democracy and education,* New York: The Free Press.

Drummond-Young, M. and Mohide, E. (2001), 'Developing problems for use in problem-based learning', in Rideout, E. *Transforming nursing education through problem-based learning.* Mississauga: Jones and Bartlett.

Gibbon, C. (2000), 'Preparation for implementing problem-based learning', in Glen, S. and Wilke, K., *Problem-based learning in nursing,* London: Macmillan.

Hafler, J. (1991), 'Case writing: case *writers'* perspectives', in Boud, D. and Felette, G. *The challenge of problem-based learning,* London: Kogan Page.

Acknowledgements

I wish to thank colleagues at the Centre for Learning and Teaching at the University of Wolverhampton, UK, the Learning Co-ordinator, Wendy Moran, who gave time, encouragement and support in other ways, and the University Print Department.

2

Demonstrating professional skills through scenario-based learning

Sandra Gammer

Introduction

As a Nursing lecturer within an undergraduate nursing programme I have the responsibility to facilitate the amalgamation of theory with practice, to prepare student nurses to develop and exercise reflection, critical thinking, and professional judgement in order for them to practise appropriately in context in their forthcoming careers as Registered Nurses.

Scenario-based learning was a medium I chose to enable third-year student nurses within the programme to develop and demonstrate professional skills required for clinical practice. I used SBL to replicate common clinical situations and thus enable my students to learn and demonstrate professional nursing skills.

Context

SBL was incorporated into the practical laboratory session, in which theory is related to practice. The scenario provides the clinical context within which the students are taught the application of theory to practice, and required to actively demonstrate it.

Scenario-based learning enables students to demonstrate their understanding, theoretical base, and application of a practical skill. In analysing the facets of a scenario, students attend to the components of the professional skill required. They essentially have to explain the 'how', 'why', and implications of their actions.

Professional skills cannot be demonstrated from theory alone. Theory guides practice, and practice directs theory. SBL enables both concepts to be demonstrated. A scenario imitating a clinical situation empowers students with experience they can transfer into practice.

New learning requires systematic development. Using a jigsaw as an analogy, the student can develop knowledge and professional skills in pieces by working through the scenario. Through scenario questions the theoretical components develop and can be transferred into the professional skill. These pieces can be systematically put together, linking the theory to practice. SBL enables the student to practise a procedure prior to performing it in 'real' life. As a result, students can assess what was expected of them, develop professional skills, and gain some confidence before going out into practice.

The 15 students in the group had two years of previous nursing training to draw upon. They had gained from their educational experience, but still required guidance and encouragement to expand their critical thinking.

This chapter is divided into three sections. The first section discusses the construction and the implementation of SBL using co-operative learning, reflection and assessment to support the student to develop and demonstrate professional skills. The second section evaluates the process of using SBL. The final section offers suggestions for educators contemplating the use of SBL.

Constructing and implementing SBL

Demonstrating professional skills requires the amalgamation of theory with practice, so the learning objectives needed to reflect this amalgamation. The learning objectives were modelled through 'critical thinking' questions addressing the scenario. The student's responses were documented in his or her scenario workbook. The students were required to embark on co-operative learning, peer-and self-assessment to encourage the development of professional skills within the scenario.

SBL – the learning objectives

- Identify the physiological responses for maintaining fluid balance
- List the contributing factors to a fluid imbalance
- Undertake an assessment of Mrs Jones' health status
- Identify through demonstration the objective and subjective assessment of Mrs Jones
- Identify and obtain the relevant resources, and administer intravenous fluids.

Students were asked to work collaboratively in self-selected groups of three. I deliberately chose three as this replicated the clinical relationship between student nurse, patient, and Registered Nurse. In a bid to authenticate the clinical situation, one student was to play the scenario patient, Mrs Jones, one the nurse and one the observer. The observer's role was to give written and verbal feedback to the nurse regarding her interaction with and care of Mrs Jones. The students were to rotate roles. They were to work co-operatively through the preliminary theoretical questions within the scenario workbook and then individually demonstrate the practical skill. The use of self- and peer-assessment was to assist in the development of their practice.

The Scenario

Mrs Jones is 82. She has experienced three-days of lethargy and malaise. Her diagnosis is dehydration requiring intravenous fluid replacement.

This scenario replicates an authentic patient problem, and is not bound to a specific clinical environment. The scenario deliberately lacks detail to encourage the student to think as laterally and as comprehensively as possible. The scenario requires the student to assess, plan and deliver individualised care for Mrs Jones.

Set scenario questions were identified within the scenario workbook. They had to be completed and investigated using a co-operative learning and reflective process. This process had been explained to the students at the beginning of the laboratory session. The questions encouraged the student to link the biological, psychological and social domains of nursing to the clinical application.

During the laboratory session I also posed further questions generated by the students' responses to the set questions. I wanted to assess their application of theory to practice and expand on it as much as possible. It was my intention that the students answer the first question as part of a formative assessment; that is, to see if they were capable of reaching conclusions in a co-operative manner and to assess the depth of their knowledge. This assessment also indicated whether or not I had to modify the structure within SBL. I was able to assess whether the structure of the scenario workbook would systematically trigger the students into exploring every possibility within Mrs Jones' clinical picture. Fortunately, the assessment was favourable.

An example of some of the questions and students' responses follows.

Scenario question 1
- What could be the possible cause of Mrs Jones' lethargy and malaise?

Each group was given five minutes to brainstorm their suggestions in their scenario workbook. Thereafter, they were asked to share their suggestions with the wider group. Various potential causes were identified, such as: a viral infection; gastro-enteritis; unable to care for herself; no family or social service support; diabetes; and bowel obstruction.

From this first exercise it was apparent that the students were comfortable working collaboratively, they were able to share their suggestions and take an active role in the discussion. From their suggestions it was evident the students were drawing on past knowledge from lectures and previous clinical experience. The realities of clinical practice require a combination of both.

To extend the critical thinking and encourage the students to concentrate on Mrs Jones I asked the following question:

"What other factors may contribute to Mrs Jones' condition? How might you assertain these?"

I wanted to challenge the students to move away from a medical focus, to think 'outside the square'. It took some prompting and a suggestion from myself before students volunteered factors that could contribute to Mrs Jones' condition, such as: self neglect; bad diet; poor hygiene standards (which could be attributed to poor eyesight). We had now progressed some way towards viewing the holistic needs of Mrs Jones.

My own professional knowledge and experience allowed me to develop and expand the students' critical thinking through the additional questions I asked.

The students were asked to add their learning to their workbook, thus supplying more revision notes. Thereafter they were given 50 minutes in their group to complete the remaining questions, and were again brought together for group discussion.

Scenario question 2
• How might you assess Mrs Jones' dehydration?

The students suggested, "*an assessment of Mrs Jones' mouth*".
From this response I asked:

"Why would you look at it, and what would you expect to find?"

The discussion took us to assessing a 'normal' and a dry tongue. The students used each other to assess a 'normal' tongue. This led us through a practical exercise of assessing the mouth, and on to discussing age-related changes occurring in the mouth. In response to a question asked by a student, which was: *"How might we assess degrees of dehydration in our patients?"*, we expanded our discussion to the clinical assessment of degrees of dehydration in our patients, to physiological changes of dehydration, and how they present. The students discussed assessment of the skin, eyes, elimination, and cardiovascular system. This range of answers once again reflected the varying depths of knowledge and experience amongst the students. What was evident was the learning taking place, the self-acknowledgement and reinforcement of knowledge. Some students were concerned about their limited knowledge, hastily documenting new findings in the scenario workbook.

The questions were developing students' cognitive understanding. However, they needed to be able to link this critical thinking and knowledge to the practice setting. SBL facilitated this link. The same format continued for question 3. For questions 4 and 5 the students were asked to demonstrate the linking of theory to practice by way of an assessment of Mrs Jones. Question 6 asked them to demonstrate the associated practical skill of intravenous fluid administration.

In addition to the set scenario questions, the scenario handbook contained a diagram of the equipment needed for the practical skill, and a self/peer-assessment table of the steps required to demonstrate the preparation of intravenous fluids and their administration to Mrs Jones. This assisted the students in developing and assessing their link between their professional knowledge and skills.

To authenticate the required assessment of Mrs Jones' health status the students were asked to role play the clinical situation. One student played Mrs Jones, one her nurse and one the observer/assessor. Through this exercise the students developed and demonstrated their professional skills. Even though Mrs Jones was role played by a healthy student, the 'actor' nurse who assessed her demonstrated the assessment procedure, and verbally described what might be seen in Mrs Jones' condition. The peer student playing Mrs Jones empathised with Mrs Jones' circumstance and explained to her "nurse" how she was feeling, and how she felt during the assessment procedure.

SBL enabled the most appropriate realistic clinical situation to be replicated within an educational environment. The students found this valuable; they stated *"It may not be as authentic as the ward but it's great to practise skills prior to performing them in 'real' life".*

SBL enabled them to practise and assess their abilities, place their learning into context and identify areas requiring further development.

Scenario question 6
- Identify and obtain the relevant resources and administer intravenous fluids (additional application of theory to practice).

The students were asked to label the diagram, held in their handbook, of the equipment necessary for administering intravenous fluids to Mrs Jones. Then they had to obtain that equipment. Some students quickly acquired the equipment, while others forgot some aspects of it. However, they had the diagram and each other to guide them. Some returned to the cupboard and in time obtained a complete set of equipment. This exercise gave them maximum opportunities to become visually familiar with the equipment, and thus the learning progressed.

Because a number of the students had little or no experience of administering intravenous fluids, I performed the following four-step demonstration. The first three steps gave maximum visual exposure of the skill and progressively linked the theory to practice before the students demonstrated the procedure themselves.

The four-step demonstration process

1. The procedure is watched by the students as I demonstrate the skill in silence
2. I repeat the skill, explaining the principles of each step
3. The students talk me through each step of the procedure, explaining the principles and rationale for each step
4. Each student performs the skill, and explains the principles and rationale to subgroup members.

With the given demonstration, the equipment diagram, and the self/peer practical assessment form, the students had a visual and written account of their practice. They commented that they felt they now had enough experience and information to continue to learn in a self-directed way.

In conclusion, the scenario replicated the professional clinical environment and enabled the students to practise and demonstrate particular clinical skills. SBL supplied a means to include complementary teaching and learning strategies, such as reflection and co-operative learning. Collectively, these approaches were instrumental in maximising the students' opportunity to develop, demonstrate and assess their professional skills.

Co-operative learning

The appeal of using co-operative learning within SBL was the collaborative teaching and learning opportunities it offered the student (Johnson and Johnson, 1981:454–458; Johnson, Johnson, Roy and Zaidman, 1985:303–321). Through demonstration of their professional skill, the students exchanged knowledge, articulated their own grasp of the subject, and taught and learnt from each other. Being exposed to other students' views and opinions, they were encouraged to accept or refute them, but were asked to explain their rationale for their alternative view. Members of groups with positive dynamics were at ease offering positive and constructive feedback to each other. These attributes were fundamental in promoting a safe environment for the students to demonstrate their knowledge and skills to each other.

Travers, Elliot and Kratochwill (1993) suggest that without support, encouragement and respect for each other the students may not feel sufficiently secure to risk presenting their opinions or actions.

Evaluating the process of SBL

Using reflection in SBL encourages students to self-examine, self-assess and evaluate their own practice (Watson, 1991:1117–1121). Without reflecting, the student is at risk of practising in a manner built of unquestioned routines, accepted directives and/or rote learning. It was evident within our discussions of reflection that a number of students believed that reflection entailed a superficial pondering of their day's activities.

They talked about 'thinking about what they were going to do, or had done'. There was no discussion on the consequences of their findings.

In order for the students to demonstrate sound professional skill and individualised patient care in caring for Mrs Jones, I encouraged them to practise a conscious three-stage analytical process of reflection; that is:

1. to reflect before acting: to critique whether their initial decisions and actions are going to be contextually appropriate. This may prevent the student from committing unnecessary errors (Greenwood, 1998:1048–1053).
2. to reflect in action: to monitor their actions during the event, in order to maintain contextually appropriate practice.
3. to reflect on action: to critically review the actions after the event – a step which is likened to evaluation (Andrews, 1996:508–513). Reflection on action usually depends on recall. Within SBL this relied on the students' self-assessment and formative feedback.

This exercise resulted in consistency of critical reflection by the group. The students demonstrated good, contextually appropriate nursing care. It prompted peer questions and personal reflection. For example, I overheard a discussion between two students as to whether Mrs Jones should be weighed, to try and ascertain if she had lost weight as a result of her illness. This was encouraging to hear, because weighing a patient is a common nursing practice, and thus at risk of being performed without a necessary motive.

The essence of the students' discussion follows

Student 1.
"I am going to ask Mrs Jones about her dietary habits, and think I will weigh her."

Student 2
"Why weigh her?"

Student 1
"I want to assess whether she has lost weight since her illness."

Student 2.
"Mrs Jones looks a healthy size, do you think weighing her will make a difference to the care she needs, which is fluid replacement?"

Student 1
"It may not; however, she is 82 and may have some degree of cardiac insufficiency, and weighing is the most accurate method of assessing body fluid status."

Student 2.
"Yes, but we are going to give her intravenous fluids, and she may present with symptoms of heart failure before we detect a significant weight increase."

This conversation continued by discussing the signs and symptoms of heart failure. This small example identifies the critical analysis and growth of discussion undertaken by the students in order for them to practise appropriately in context. This depth of critical reflection and discussion was evident in the majority of students. One problem I identified with the reflective process was that on occasions I had to guide and prevent some students from over questioning to such a degree that they lost sight of the central issue, moving into an entirely different concept. Some students scrutinised their every decision within the scenario.

Student perspectives

Generally the students were very receptive to SBL. They appreciated working through a clinically relevant scenario. The vast majority liked working co-operatively; they found they could learn a great deal from each other.

A range of their comments follows:

" Really appreciated learning a subject relevant and important to my practice."
"It was good to practise the skill prior to going out into the wards."
"I now know what I do and do not know."
"I know what I have to do to develop myself."
"I enjoyed the role play."
"I could practice my teaching skills."
"Having the workbook means I can revisit it whenever I want to."

Benefits of implementing SBL within the Bachelor of Nursing Programme

- SBL encourages students to question the appropriateness of their knowledge and actions and facilitates the use of reflection and critical thinking. The value of critical thinking is that it can guide students to move away from focusing on one way of practising, or from needing to find only one right answer, toward beginning to assess and evaluate the contextual appropriateness of their actions (Kessinich, Guyatt and DiCenso, 1997: 25–29).

- Through critical thinking, students can critically assess their learning, and thereafter take responsibility for their own professional development.
- SBL offers the student a contextual means to practise and develop new and existing skills.
- If the students make mistakes during this simulated exercise, they can learn from this, and at the same time feel safe that their simulated actions are, in effect, harmless.
- SBL gave me free time to converse with the co-operative groups during the scenario.
- SBL gave me time to give support, guidance and feedback to the students, and to formatively assess their strengths and limitations.

Challenges of SBL in the bachelor of nursing programme

The challenges were not the direct result of scenario-based learning, but associated with the complementary teaching and learning strategies I used within SBL.

- Within the co-operative group there is scope for unequal participation. Outlining and discussing roles and responsibilities of the group members can guide the students to demonstrate their accountability and to work co-operatively and effectively.
- Some students may have limited experience to draw upon, and may not be able to recognise the consequences of their decisions or actions in order to modify or change these. Co-operative learning, reflection and formative assessment can develop this ability.
- Some students may find working with unfamiliar students intimidating. Allowing them to self-select their group may assist them in obtaining some comfort and support from their peers.
- The students may not feel safe to openly express their reflections or feedback comments. Teaching the students appropriate ways to share positive and constructive feedback can assist them to feel sufficiently secure to present their opinions without fear of criticism (Travers, Elliott and Kratochwill *et al.*, 1993).
- Some groups may work through the scenario too hastily. Spending time discussing the scenario and its questions with the group can prompt and guide them to be more thorough in their responses.

Suggestions for educators wishing to use SBL

- Take time to clearly explain and discuss the aims and structure of SBL to your students. This will contribute positively to its effective implementation. This is time well spent!
- Because a number of desirable attributes may be necessary within a given scenario, the learning objectives, scenario questions and assessment must enable the student to demonstrate all of these attributes (Hager, Gonzi and Athanasom, 1994: 3–16).
- When designing the scenario, the learning outcomes, assessment, scenario and its

supporting components all need to be clear, realistic and attainable for the students. Otherwise their ability to manage a task appropriately in a demanding and/or complex environment, or extend the application to a different situation or context can be limited (Toohey, Ryan and Hughes, 1996: 215–227).

- Foster and role-model positive and constructive feedback. In so doing we can facilitate enthusiasm, and the recurrence of positive behaviour from our students (Skinner, 1971).

Conclusion

Scenario-based learning facilitates the integration of theory with practice within the Bachelor of Nursing programme. It supports a diversity of learning and assessment strategies. Students thus encouraged to use reflection and formative assessment in a conscious and calculated fashion can assess their own learning, place their learning into context and evaluate the contextual appropriateness of their actions.

If the educational environment is supportive and strives to build a relationship of mutual respect and trust between students and the educator, the students will feel secure sharing their initiatives in a co-operative manner, teaching and learning from each other. Scenario-based learning has surpassed my expectations for fostering an inquiring and co-operative learner.

References

Andrews, M. (1996), 'Using reflection to develop clinical expertise', *British Journal of Nursing*, vol.5, no.8, pp.508–513.

Greenwood, J. (1998), 'The role of reflection in single and double loop learning', *Journal of Advanced Nursing*, vol. 27, pp.1048–1053.

Hager, P. Gonzi, A. and Athanasom, A. (1994), 'General issues about assessment & competence', *Assessment & Evaluation in Higher Education*, vol.19, no.1, pp.3–16.

Johnson, D. and Johnson, R. (1981), 'Effects of cooperative and individualistic learning and inter-ethnic interaction', *Journal of Educational Psychology*, vol.73, no.3, pp.454–459.

Johnson, D., Johnson, R., Roy, P. and Zaidman, B. (1985), 'Oral interaction in cooperative learning groups: Speaking, listening, and the nature of statements made by high-, medium- and low-achieving students', *The Journal of Psychology*, vol. 119, no. 4, pp.303–321.

Kessinich, K., Guyatt, G.H. and DiCenso, A. (1997), 'Teaching nursing students evidence based nursing', *Nurse Educator*, vol. 22, no.6, pp.25–29 Nov/Dec.

Skinner, B. F. (1971), *Beyond freedom & dignity*, New York: Knopf.

Toohey, S., Ryan, C. and Hughes, C. (1996), 'Assessing the practicum', *Assessment & Evaluation in Higher Education*, vol, 21, no.3, pp.215–227.

Travers, J., Elliott, S. and Kratochwill, T. (1993), *Educational psychology: Effective teaching, effective learning*, Wisconsin-Madison: Brown & Benchmark.

Watson, S. (1997), 'An analysis of the concept of experience', *Journal of Advanced Nursing*, vol.16, pp.1117–1121.

3

Developing reflective practice through scenario-based learning

Kim van Wissen

Introduction

Reflective practice is a way of working and developing professionally (Rolfe, 1998; Rolfe, Freshwater and Jasper, 2001) and has been used by nurses for the last decade. It entails the mental exercise of reflection by looking systematically at one's own work practice (Rolfe, Freshwater and Jasper, 2001). All professionals reflect on their day's work, but reflective practice aims to employ these reflections as a means of learning and progressing within the environment that a professional (nurse) works.

Encouraging a class of postgraduate nurses to use reflective practice requires a very practical method of teaching. Scenario-based learning (SBL) provides this method, as it marries the theoretical classroom learning with the clinical work situation for the students. Effectively, scenario-based learning helps clarify the complexity of the human predicament and human interactions within which nursing is sited.

The aim of the following exploration is to express some of the issues that I encountered when using SBL for the purposes of reflective practice. I consider how SBL is an effective process for contextual teaching. I also look at how SBL allows the principles of classroom learning to be applied to the work environment. Finally in this chapter, I outline some of the practical issues associated with SBL as I encountered them. These include specifics about the scenario, the use of journals and SBL, comments on students' ability to cope with a new learning process, and also suggestions for prospective SBL users/facilitators when considering this approach for themselves.

Scenario-based learning: a focus on context

The student group

The postgraduate students on which this exploration is based are mature, experienced nurses who at the time had been in clinical practice for at least five years. The six members of the group had met each other before on other postgraduate papers. Hereafter I label these postgraduate nurses 'students'.

The learning intention

Reflective practice in nursing involves the ability of nurses to reflect critically upon their work/professional environment and learn from this experience. The process itself can be transforming in some minor or major way. Nurse leaders suggest that reflection may not necessarily be transforming but at least it may bring about a self-awareness in nurses (Lumby, 1998). This is important for advancing nursing knowledge and can enable nurses to transcend ill-informed rituals and routines of their daily practice.

I specifically wanted to facilitate the process of reflective practice and use this approach as a template that could be used at any time and anywhere concepts in the classroom were specifically relevant to the practice environment. I hoped that these students would begin to question their work and even make changes following critical reflection on their practice.

The first scenario

The first scenario I presented to students in class involved them having to diffuse a family argument on a ward. In my role as 'nurse', I had to ask family members to leave the patient's cubicle as they were disrupting care of both their mother and other patients. The following scenario was presented to the class via an overhead projection:

Scenario One

There was a lot of noise coming from a two-bedded cubicle I was attending to that evening. I went to see what was going on, and found one family and the patient they had come to see arguing forcefully. I asked them if they could perhaps continue the discussion elsewhere. The family argument continued outside the ward; the husband and son debating if treatment should continue for the dying wife/mother. I joined the family outside the ward to ask if I could answer any questions. Half an hour later they seemed happier – their main concern was about pain relief, which I could easily address.

The scenario to which the students were required to relate encompassed some major issues: death and dying, and coping with family needs. After recounting the scenario, the students were asked which three overarching questions would be useful to ask of any scenario. In response, students came up with the following three questions:

• Why is this an important situation to consider?
• What would you do?
• Why would you do that?

These questions provided a useful framework for contextually analysing scenarios in class. By using the scenario as a platform, these questions gave students a springboard to improve their critical thinking for reflective practice. The contexts they related to, and reflected on, were multiple: the physical context was the ward environment; the emotional context involved them working through the grieving process; and the professional context prompted the need for effective communication.

One aspect of SBL, which I noted throughout my experience, was the need to focus on a scenario in such a way that a clear context was determined, becoming a point of reference. The context of the scenario became pivotal for students' ability to apply explicit abstract ideas or issues. For example in Scenario One, I asked the students to simply identify emergent ethical issues and then reflect upon them. The students recognised and acknowledged the many issues (for example, power over control of patient, and culture and care) surrounding the complexity of 'care'.

This in turn emphasises a further attribute of SBL: I used scenarios taken from 'real' practice as these scenarios often seemed simple and uncomplicated to students at first glance. By using SBL, students revealed numerous features that had not been considered relevant to a particular case before, so what seemed initially uncomplicated was revealed to be quite the opposite. Through scenario-based learning students came to realise that they needed to develop analytical skills which they could apply to different circumstances in a systematic manner. No two patients are the same and SBL allowed students to explore the composite life of the patient.

Scenario-based learning was used to shift the focus of learning away from core curriculum content (Janing, 1997) towards seemingly more incidental or peripheral notions that were introduced by students as part of their reflection. Scenarios elevated their need to know about the minutiae of the professional context. Often this detail gave rise to ethical debates and judgements: students realised that keeping the context of a patient's life in mind involved making difficult or even controversial clinical decisions.

Returning to Scenario One, I asked students to reflect on how the scenario might have proceeded if

a)   a nurse had intervened before the argument had time to escalate; or
b)   a nurse had not diffused the arguing at all.

The comments made by students were extremely varied, but subsequent discussion served to accentuate how professional judgement was exercised by nurses in the work environment. Students became more able to reflect from the standpoint of being a nurse, and also an adult learner (Foley, 2000). Class debate centred on the need for professional practitioners to monitor themselves (Heron, 1989). It also alerted students to how their actions impacted upon others (Foley, 2000), especially in terms of the nurse–patient relationship. This exercise gave students many insights into their own practice. More importantly they appeared more perceptive about how their peers also made professional judgements.

Another satisfying aspect of SBL was the heightened development of self-directed learning (Dearmun, 2000) generated by specific scenarios. One could argue that these postgraduate students were self-motivated (Lefrancois, 1994), hence self-directed learning was a natural progression. My main observation was that SBL directed students to source information in innovative ways, stimulated by the discussions initiated in the construction of the presented scenario. Students continued analysing the scenarios outside the classroom, and a case would often provide a framework for their own course assignment work. For example, one student used the three 'stock' questions as a framework for her two written assignments, explaining why she chose this questioning process at the outset.

SBL: between the classroom and the real world

Reflective practitioners also need to be critical thinkers (Atkins, 2000; Taylor, 2000). The postgraduate students needed to develop particular characteristics pertaining to critical thinking in their practice by:

- acquiring a strong sense of self-awareness
- learning to critically analyse their work environment
- exploring their feelings in a constructive manner
- questioning the status quo
- considering relevant innovative options to improve or change the work environment.

To explore these characteristics, scenario details were sent to students a week before each block course day. Before attending class, the students needed time to consider a given scenario and answer the 'stock' questions developed previously. Scenario Two is the one that was sent to students at home.

Scenario Two

Please reflect upon a critical incident that has occurred at your place of work either recently or in the distant past.
    The working definition of a critical incident is:
    An observable human activity which presents itself as an important or significant episode, and affords analysis.
    Please write down your reflections.
    Also answer the three 'stock' questions as usual.

To promote greater self-awareness, I asked students to describe their own critical incident (Preskill, 1997; Smith, 1998; Tripp, 1993) on paper. I did this so that students would be able to use a scenario extracted from their work setting, thus making the process of critical reflection more relevant to their own practice. For example, one student described an incident where she gave an intra-muscular injection and actually felt the needle-end hit the patient's bone. Her story was emotive and descriptive, neither critical nor analytical. I asked the students to think about this incident and apply their 'stock' questions to the scenario. By using the scenario presented by the student, the postgraduates were moved beyond simple description and became more aware of how the incident/scenario provided a learning experience. The student who had recounted the incident explained how she had then discussed the effect of the needle on the bone with medical staff. She had even made inquiries about available research on this matter from the manufacturer of the syringe equipment.

As an educator I needed to assist students in making the intellectual leap from classroom knowledge to their real workplace setting. Scenario-based learning provided this platform. We used the scenario as a kernel of issues and concepts that we could then 'unpack' together. The most successful kind of scenario, from which students gained most insight came directly from someone's nursing practice, rather than being one I had prefabricated myself.

Scenario-based learning: an evaluation

In the following section I offer some points of evaluation that were significant in my use of SBL with the postgraduate group.

Prepared versus unprepared scenarios

The scenario I prepared for use with any given class provided a good starting point for developing an unambiguous trajectory for discussion. However, because I was teaching a postgraduate group, these students often had excellent scenarios from which to draw upon. As a facilitator, I had to learn quickly which of the scenarios had the most potential for achieving learning needs.

A further aspect of the facilitator's role involved allowing students to make outlandish suggestions about issues or offer nonconformist solutions to problems that emerged within the scenario. We call this 'going into orbit'– designed to generate more creative learning. The three 'stock' questions allowed the students to 'go into orbit' to explore what the scenario was aiming to teach them. However, in retrospect, SBL is only as good as the scenario presented. I needed to acquire considerable confidence in predicting how the scenario would meet the learning outcomes. There were numerous occasions when I miscalculated the direction of discussion and analysis for both prepared and unprepared scenarios. As this approach to learning is more adventurous, highly productive periods are often coupled with redundant episodes.

The scenarios of student origin always achieved the desired outcome (making students think). I believe that this was so because students had ownership of the 'incident' and therefore ownership of the critique.

Pushing students beyond their comfort-zone

Scenario-based learning as a process facilitated students' thinking outside the square by encouraging them to make new/original theoretical connections. This is precisely what reflective practitioners should also be doing. Students were asked to look at their practice from a perspective they would not normally consider in order to demonstrate the need for openness towards innovations. Students were given Scenario Three:

Scenario Three

You have come in to see your patient after the afternoon report.

Dan
- is young
- is on the ward for six-hourly intravenous antibiotics
- has dark circles under his eyes
- keeps yawning
- tells you he is tired and can't focus on his reading.

Dan is getting a good night's sleep while he is in hospital so please do not include lack of sleep in your assessment and diagnosis.

- What is your nursing assessment and diagnosis?
- Why?

Using Scenario Three, students were asked to make their assessments and arrive at a nursing diagnosis. Students had to present an alternative insight, and were asked to defend their diagnosis in a debate format to the class. The class then decided which arguments were the most convincing. In this way students were forced to consider options they would probably have ignored in reality. There were some interesting diagnostic suggestions, all of which were quite plausible:

- He had cancer and had just received chemotherapy.
- He had taken too many sleeping pills.
- He had commenced taking new medication.
- He had been taking antihistamine tablets that made him drowsy.
- The dark circles around the eyes were due to a chronic allergy.

This exercise not only drew attention to ingrained practitioner assumptions but also compelled students to remember that they must investigate all possibilities, both in establishing the origin of the problem and then in making clinical decisions about its treatment.

The aforementioned elements are central to critical thinking and consequent reflective practice as taught in the classroom environment. Students were also asked to undertake critical self-directed learning by keeping a written reflective journal (Rolfe, Freshwater and Jasper, 2001; Taylor, 2000).

Journalling as an adjunct to scenario-based learning

Using the reflective journal (Abegglen and O'Neill Conger, 1997), students develop their ability to move from descriptions of their practice to critically thinking through the incidents of their practice on paper. This is the essence of good critical thinking using the reflective journal (Rolfe, Freshwater and Jasper, 2001).

I was impressed with the high level of self-directed scenario-based learning evident in most journals (Duke, 2000) written by the postgraduate nurses. At one point during the semester I reviewed the journals. Surprisingly, students were doing two things simultaneously: first, they were analysing genuine critical incidents (scenarios); and second, they were reflecting on reflecting. The scenarios written by students tended to identify and analyse similar themes. These themes established the students' ability to incorporate critical thinking and professional nursing standards into one activity (Abegglen and O'Neill Congèr, 1997). Journal themes included:

- questioning the status quo, therefore questioning their own workplace socio-cultural beliefs
- analysing why things were the way they were, therefore analysing and appreciating the underlying work culture
- suggesting solutions to problems that arose from the scenarios they scrutinised.

These themes were exactly what I had hoped the students would examine and analyse because they are consistent with the literature describing the benefits of reflective journalling (Rolfe, Freshwater and Jasper, 2001; Taylor, 2000). In each journal, the scenario was central and was again used as a dais from which to express, in a theoretical or applied manner, how the student reflected upon their practice at that time.

So why use scenario-based learning with postgraduate students?

Scenario-based learning is an ideal learning process for postgraduate students, mainly because they have relevant prior experience to call upon. I used Scenario Four to engage students in exploring subjective feelings as part of their training in critical thinking.

Scenario Four

On a cardiac care unit two people needed urgent open-heart surgery. However, there was only room on the theatre-list to put through one case. The forty-year-old patient was chosen ahead of the eighty-four-year-old patient.
Please answer your 'stock questions as usual.
Please also answer the following questions:

1. How do I feel about this decision?
2. Why do I feel this way about the incident?
3. What are the positive aspects learned from this incident?
4. What are the negative aspects learned from this incident?

Students realised that they needed to answer the stock questions first to provide a familiar frame in which to work. The additional questions were partially covered by the 'stock' questions but not enough to explore subjective/objective feelings. The first two questions inevitably stimulated negative comments about their reaction to the circumstances. The students clearly vented their dismay at the situation, believing that the eighty-four-year-old had as much right to the surgery as the forty-year-old. The second question forced them, as reflective practitioners, to seek out the multiple layers of feelings underpinning the various circumstances in which the two patients found themselves. This meant they were required to examine the situation in a more insightful manner and also ask more functional and operational questions. Some students worked through these scenarios with ease as their clinical experience helped underpin and justify their explanations.

Scenario-based learning, as with critical thinking, leads students to question the accepted norms of behaviour (FitzGerald and Chapmann, 2000) and to identify taken-for-granted assumptions that lack substance. These students soon realised that questioning these norms would always be contentious. Using a scenario, students practised ways of communicating with co-workers so that their questioning was non-threatening and non-confrontational.

Facilitating scenario-based learning

I have arrived at the following list of observations for facilitating my own student group using SBL as a process.

- Students learned by an unpredictable and yet open mode of learning. With guidance, students more easily achieved their expected learning outcomes, particularly when using scenarios based on personal experience.
- As an educator, I learned from the students by allowing impromptu episodes of student facilitation of scenario reflection.
- Students found their roles as information seekers and receivers different from conventional discourses of learning.
- Students only gradually began to think beyond accepted recipes, and to understand that reflective practice was more than following prescribed steps.
- Student debate and conflict were nurtured by turning these processes into learning opportunities.
- What the student and the educator wished to achieve in analysing a scenario often differed from each other. I needed to be flexible about student learning needs.

As a process, scenario-based learning compelled me to abandon structured tutorials in favour of working with scenarios either students or I presented. This was not a comfortable stratagem initially but is now a way of teaching that I embrace.

Conclusion

My experiences of employing SBL have shown it to be an invaluable tool for postgraduate teaching for contextual learning and application.

- It allowed students to focus on a case or scenario so a context was clearly established.
- This context provided a platform for exploring conceptually multifarious ideas/issues.
- SBL facilitated a focus away from core curriculum requirements.
- The objectives of SBL for reflective practice purposes aimed to have students deal with a scenario and then extrapolate their findings to their own professional work environment.
- SBL allowed students to examine the scenario as a distinct entity and then to apply the observed generalisations to more specific events.
- SBL coupled with critical thinking allowed students to grow into more reflective practitioners as they mastered the skills of critique.
- The scenarios used were realistic and therefore similar to those found in the workplace.

The discussion has aimed to elucidate how scenario-based learning can be indispensable for developing critical thinking and analysis within reflective practice. There is a natural tendency for nurses to employ scenarios for synthesising situations and seeking solutions. They learn to link theoretical knowledge clearly to the context of their work. Therefore SBL is a valuable mode of teaching and learning for my postgraduate student group.

References

Abegglen, J. and O'Neill Conger, C. (1997), 'Critical thinking in nursing: classroom tactics that work', *Journal of Nursing Education*, vol. 36, no. 10, pp. 452–458.

Aitkens, S. (2000), 'Developing underlying skills in the move towards reflective practice', in Burns S. and Bulman C. (eds), *Reflective practice in nursing* (2nd ed.), Oxford: Blackwell Science.

Dearmun, N. (2000), 'The legacy of reflective practice', in Burns S. and Bulman C. (eds), *Reflective practice in nursing* (2nd ed.), Oxford: Blackwell Science.

Duke, S. (2000), 'The experience of becoming reflective', in Burns S. and Bulman C. (eds), *Reflective practice in nursing* (2nd ed.), Oxford: Blackwell Science.

FitzGerald, M. and Chapman, Y. (2000), 'Theories of reflection for learning', in Burns S. and Bulman C. (eds), *Reflective practice in nursing* (2nd ed.), Oxford: Blackwell Science.

Foley, G. (2000), *Understanding adult education and training* (2nd ed.), Sydney: Allen & Unwin.

Heron, J. (1989), *The facilitator's handbook*, London: Kogan Page.

Janing, J. (1997), 'Assessment of a scenario-based approach to facilitating critical thinking among paramedic students', *Prehospital Disaster Medicine*, vol. 12, no.3, pp.215–221.

Lefrançois , G. (1994), *Psychology for teaching: a bear always, usually, sometimes, rarely, never, always faces the front*, Belmont, California: Wadsworth.

Lumby, J. (1998), 'Transforming nursing through reflective practice', in Johns C. and Freshwater, D. (eds), *Transforming nursing through reflective practice*, Oxford: Blackwell Science.

Preskill, H. (1997), 'Using critical incidents to model effective evaluation practice in the teaching of evaluation', *Evaluation Practice*, vol. 18, pp.65–72.

Rolfe, G., Freshwater, D. and Jasper, M. (2001), *Critical reflection for nursing and the helping professions: a user's guide*, New York: Palgrave.

Rolfe, G. (1998), 'Beyond expertise: reflective and reflexive nursing practice', in Johns C. and Freshwater, D. (eds), *Transforming nursing through reflective practice*. Oxford: Blackwell Science.

Smith, A. (1998), 'Learning about reflection', *Journal of Advanced Nursing*, vol. 28, pp.891–903.

Taylor, B. J. (2000), *Reflective practice: a guide for nurses and midwives*. NSW, Australia: Allen & Unwin.

Tripp, D. (1993), *Critical incidents in teaching*, London: Routledge.

4

Paper to program: Developing a computer-based learning package for SBL

Stephen Bell and Rachel Page

Introduction

Recently we introduced our Bachelor of Health Science degree majoring in Environmental Health as an extramural offering. This meant that our papers had to be developed into an extramural mode so they could be effectively delivered off-campus. The benefit of delivering papers by distance learning was that students interested in the material did not have to travel to the university to study. However, a major cause for the high dropout rate in extramural papers is that these papers are reliant on 90–100% self-directed learning. Our main objective was to examine new and exciting ways in which we could introduce the student to course material applicable to the learning outcomes of the paper but also provide an interesting and valued learning experience.

The challenge for us was to find a way in which the distance-learning students could have the advantages of scenario-based learning that the internal students already had. We opted for developing an interactive computer program which the extramural students could practice decision-making procedures that are covered by the internal students in the classroom.

This chapter will primarily look at the steps we took to develop our selected scenario to its final delivery as a computer package. This will involve discussions on scenario selection, the development process for decision-making and the integration of these concepts by computer programmers to develop a useful, interactive, computer scenario-based learning package.

First steps in selection of scenario

Our group has been using scenario-based learning (SBL) for our internal environmental health students for at least the past seven years. SBL has provided the means for enabling the students to think critically, apply the knowledge learnt in the paper in which the scenario is based, incorporate their knowledge from other relevant papers and work together in the decision-making process. Scenarios have also been useful in providing students with access to realistic workplace situations at a time and place convenient to us. Some of the situations that environmental health professionals are involved with may be delicate, such as investigating infectious disease, or simply inconvenient to provide as learning situations for students. For example, substandard houses may be available to visit but not at the time the paper is being delivered, and there is also the ethical issue regarding privacy of the occupants and exposing them to a whole raft of enquiring students. Finally, extramural students do not have the same access to professional contacts and consequently might well miss out on this type of situation in real life.

With environmental health work there are sometimes many avenues to take, and which one is chosen often depends on the particular situation and on the judgement of the individual environmental health officer. The scenarios chosen for our internal papers have tended to be based on real events and situations that environmental health officers or health protection officers have had to deal with. This has made the scenario-based learning real and applicable to the students and has also allowed them to compare their decisions with those made by the participants in the real-life event.

Before we embarked on investigating appropriate software for establishing an interactive computer program for scenario-based learning we needed to clarify what it was that we were trying to achieve with this approach to teaching and how it was to be delivered.

Context of the scenario

We elected to work on only one scenario with the premise that once we sorted out developing the interactive program for one, it would be easier to apply these principles to further scenarios. We already had the expertise and case scenarios available for making this interactive computer program range across several papers. We focused on the 200-level Environmental Health Law paper for development of a computer-assisted case scenario learning package. The main reason for this was that the scenarios available to us were relatively straightforward in comparison to other papers.

In the Environmental Health Law paper we require the student to use and interpret law. We therefore needed to choose an interesting and realistic scenario that the student would be likely to come across in their working environment. The scenario we finally selected for development into an interactive decision-making program involved the students putting themselves in the position of visiting a substandard house. They had to report on the condition of the house, and select the appropriate law to deal with the conditions they encountered. The students needed to identify the correct legal solutions relating to the situation and the correct procedures in dealing with the people involved.

Development of the scenario-based computer package

The aim of our task was to devise an interactive computer program that would take the students through a scenario and make it real and relevant. More importantly, the program had to be designed such that the students would learn decision-making processes: how to integrate the knowledge they had already learnt in the paper and apply it to a real event.

We asked ourselves "How can we achieve this scenario-based learning using a computer package?" It was a difficult task. We needed to be realistic with what we could deliver and had to identify certain points that were essential for the program to work. First, the interactive program had to operate without a lecturer's guidance. Second, the program needed to provide feedback for the students accessing the scenario. This feedback could be immediate during the scenario or at the completion of the scenario. Both types of feedback were essential for the students to know what consequences resulted from the decisions they made. Third, the computer program had to reflect a real situation for the students, otherwise they would not even try or continue with the package, Finally, the program had to be suitable and adaptable for online learning, so that the extramural students had access to this scenario-based computer program.

We decided that the best approach was to develop the scenario first before launching into software purchase. We felt that once we knew what we wanted to do and how to do it, the software purchase and use would be more straightforward. The steps we took for developing the interactive computer program follow:

1) Identifying and selecting the scenario(s)
2) Working through a scenario
3) Deciding on a computer program
4) Testing and evaluation.

1.   Identifying and selecting the scenario(s)

Having decided on developing a single scenario that was appropriate for the Environmental Health Law paper, we wanted to create a realistic one, so the first step was to brainstorm some ideas. This was made easier in that some scenarios from previous class studies were already in existence. Once we had a framework, we needed to make sure that all our learning outcomes were defined and covered in the exercise. We settled on the scenario of the substandard house so that the students could practise house inspection techniques in a relatively comfortable learning environment. Each scenario in reality is quite different, but the methodology used to investigate these situations is quite straightforward and applicable under many circumstances. Inspections of premises need to be structured and to follow a logical pattern if errors and omissions are to be avoided. By using this scenario we were both supporting learning of the paper's content, the law, and providing the student with reinforcement of inspection techniques learned elsewhere. Being able to evaluate a situation, assess the risk and deal with the issues appropriately is a critical part of the Environmental Health 'toolbox'.

2.   Working through the scenario

There are implications in working through and developing scenario-based learning for a computer that do not apply in a classroom situation. For many scenarios that occur in the classroom the students can interact with each other and the teacher and be guided in how the scenario evolves. In a computer program you don't have that interactive opportunity unless it is built-in. Hence it is important to go through the decision-making process thoroughly. Once the scenario had been identified we had to consider

Figure 4.1 Scenario development

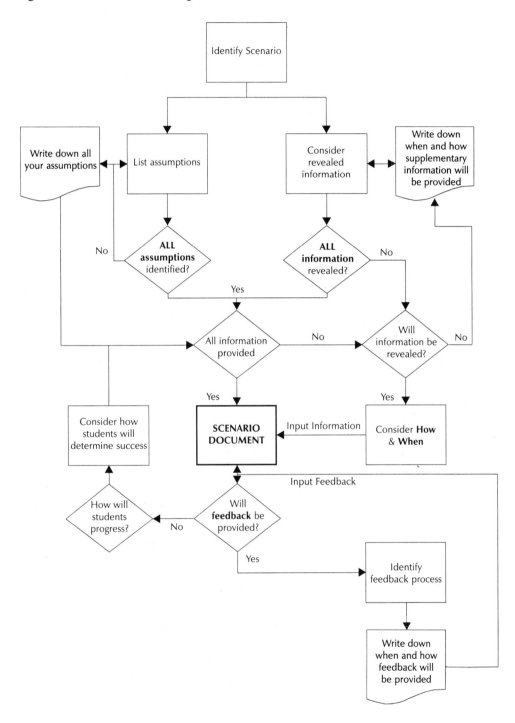

Stephen Bell & Dr Rachel Page

assumptions, revelation of information, and feedback processes. As we have said, much of this is implicit in the classroom and you can develop as you go along, but with a computer program this has to be more carefully considered and constructed. So development of the scenario involved determining specific pathways, mapping of these pathways and identifying interlinks and relationships between the pathways mapped. The whole process we followed is shown in Figure 4.1, Scenario Development; however this is made up of three parts, Dealing with Information (Figure 4.2), Delivering Supplementary Information (Figure 4.3) and Providing Feedback (Figure 4.4), which are examined individually, along with developmental issues that arose as we progressed.

Dealing with information

The first step here was to consider any assumptions, and spell them out. When you are in a classroom you have the luxury of discussing issues as they arise, but in the scenario-based learning situation you need to anticipate every possibility, even the ones from left field. We needed to make the computer program able to cope with this. So we put ourselves in the position of an outsider being asked to undertake this process or case scenario. We were in the position to do this as two members of the team involved in developing the interactive computer scenario-based learning program were not familiar with the course material of the Environmental Health Law paper.

We created a scenario and then asked ourselves what assumptions we had made about the students' ability and knowledge, and what we wanted them to develop. So we listed our assumptions and what we wanted the students to "discover". This is shown in Figure 4.2, Deal with Information, part of our flow chart in Figure 4.1.

We also needed to ask how this scenario would arise in the workplace. We needed to consider how investigators would have found out about the situation; what they would have done to prepare for the visit; items they could, or should have taken; how they travelled to the place concerned; and the variety of responses and conditions they might have encountered. We tried role-play gaming (RPG) techniques to develop and extend this learning process. What these techniques do is present a scenario to the "player", and a number of decisions – each decision has a consequence, some lead to dead ends, others progress the "player" through the game. We intended to follow the same process. So the initial brief outlined in the scenario was *'How did the student come to hear of the situation we were presenting?'* Starting at the very beginning and not part-way through meant we didn't make critical errors or unreasonable assumptions about the students' understanding of the scenario. Each student was then expected to make some decisions as to how next to proceed. For example, in the extract from the written instructions shown as Scenario Instructions Extract 1, we anticipated a range of options and responses from students. The students were required to select items to take with them when they visited the substandard house. They were also asked for a justification for why they chose particular items. Their responses and decisions for this step were recorded and displayed at the end of the scenario for the student to reflect on. Note that in this example and the others that follow, the text in italics is for the programmer, and will not be seen by the student. It is how we discriminated between programming instructions and program content.

Scenario Instructions: Extract 1
Pre-inspection procedures

Before you visit the house there are some things you need to do; these include checking your diary to select a time and date for your visit, booking a car and checking where you need to go.

Q1: What do you need to take with you?

Put a tick alongside the items you want to take with you:

ITEM	TICK REQUIRED
Notebook	✔
Pen	✔
Warrant	✔
Torch	✔ *possible*
Sample Jars	✗
Noise Level meter	✗
Thermometer	✗
Light meter	✗
Camera 35mm DX	*either/or* (✔
Polaroid Camera	(✔
Tape Measure	✔

✔ *Missing or no entry = Error message "you seem to have forgotten something - check"*
✔ *present in ✗box Error message "Why have you selected the {name}? Write your answer in the box provided"*

Write your answer here

Note: Each question is numbered in scenario instructions. Numbering made tracking them through the document (and subsequent programming) easier.

Once at the destination the student was then asked to write an initial greeting into a textbox, to be compared at the end of the exercise with a fairly standard set of expected greetings. The student was then faced with a range of responses, generated at random. The range of responses generated was based on a likely response and not a bizarre behaviour. Students were met with acceptance, hesitant acceptance or refusal. The

Figure 4.2 Dealing with information

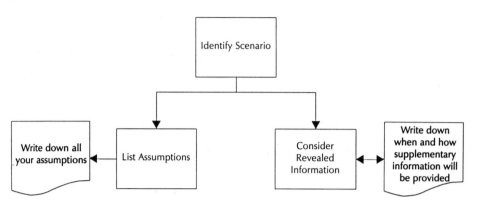

refusal put them into another activity loop which eventually permitted entry. Once inside the property, photos and text portrayed the environment. There were two versions of text they could have encountered, each requiring a specific response. Students were now provided with additional information to help them develop the overall scenario.

Delivering supplementary information

There are two sorts of information: background information, which is needed for starting the scenario; and then supplementary information, which is revealed as the scenario progresses. The background information presented to the students sets the scene for the scenario, whereas the supplementary material supports and underpins subsequent decisions. The supplementary information would normally have been disclosed in discussions in the classroom. This is all part of the Supplementary Information process shown here in Figure 4.3, Deliver Supplementary Information, again a section of the flow chart in Figure 4.1.

For revealing the supplementary information you need to consider what information the students already have and what they will need. So it is necessary to decide what will be revealed, and how and when in the scenario this supplementary information will be provided. These may be incremental steps, the amount, delivery and type of information dependent on the scenario.

Following the provision of supplementary material students were required to make further decisions. As in real life, the decisions are not clear-cut and choices are made. In the example provided, in the following Scenario Instructions: Extract 2, students can make two correct choices from four displayed. The use of a textbox provided an opportunity for justifying the decision and reflecting on it later. They were then required to reflect on and refine their answer. In this process, instant feedback is provided if their answer is incorrect with a prompt to rethink the answer or a short explanation to point them in the right direction. This is all part of the feedback process we considered critical for successful operation of this package.

Figure 4.3 Deliver supplementary information

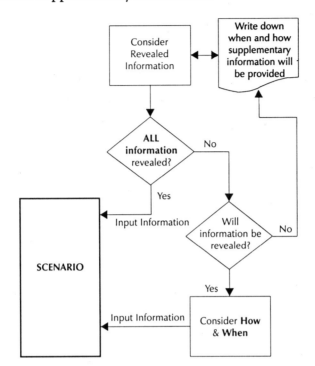

Scenario Instructions: Extract 2

Q6: What is the most appropriate Act to take action under?

You have been appointed under the following Acts; select which is the most appropriate to use in this situation.

Act	Tick one box
Building Act 1991	✔ *(optional)*
Health Act 1956	✔
Resource Management Act 1991	✗
Local Government Act 1974	✗

You may need to go away and review these Acts or some of the terms used in the inspection sheet.

At this stage the student is also provided with the ability to "save & quit or continue". This provision was made at several stages in the program, but they could not save just anywhere. Because of the variations in responses we introduced, the save/continue functions had to be restricted to specific sections so that the student would actually continue with the same scenario they started, not a subsequent variation. It was intended to allow the student to stop and seek additional information.

In the final program there was also a link to a supporting website once the save and quit had been used. We felt this was a useful adjunct to the program as it provided further information in relation to the scenario.

Providing feedback

The first step is to decide whether feedback is essential or not. If you are not going to provide feedback within the program you need to ask yourself how students are going to assess their own progress. It is likely that some form of feedback will be required, but that not all places in the scenario requiring student input require feedback. Where feedback is required you need to identify the process of feedback, the type of feedback provided and how and when it will be delivered.

We considered feedback another key point in the programme and our "feedback loop" is shown in Figure 4.4, Provide Feedback, which is derived from Figure 4.1. We chose a variety of feedback types, from immediate to delayed feedback which was displayed at the end and compared the student's answer with an exemplar. In our scenario, after the students had proceeded through the exercise they were presented with their answers and examples for comparisons. Students' responses were recorded and displayed for them to reflect and learn, and in some cases some pro-forma style letters or responses were also provided for comparison.

Figure 4.4 Provide Feedback

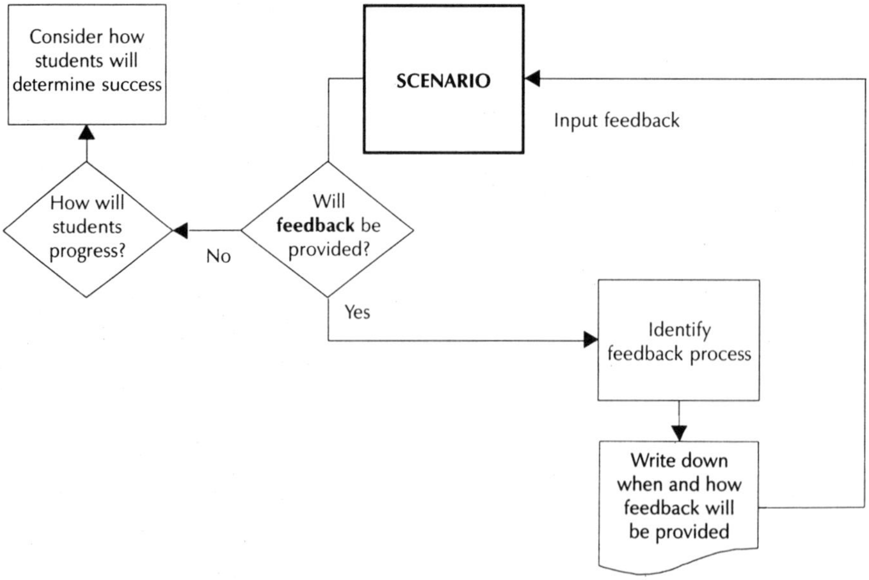

In the extracts from the scenario instructions provided earlier you can see examples of both immediate feedback – the error messages – and delayed feedback, the text or comment box. Delayed feedback also included pro-forma letters where the student's name was inserted at appropriate places within the program to personalise the response. This personal touch made the scenario more realistic and memorable to the students. The following extract from the scenario instruction (Extract 3) is an example from our hard-copy for generation of a pro-forma letter, again with instructions in italics to the programmer to introduce the personalised responses.

Scenario Instruction: Extract 3

I will visit you on {*insert live date + 11 days*} to ensure the work has been done to a satisfactory standard. If you have any difficulty undertaking this work please contact me at 555-7926 ext. 756 as soon as possible.

Yours faithfully,

{insert Student Name}
Environmental Health Officer

---

3.   *Deciding on a computer program*

Once the hard-copy for the decision process was produced based on the flow chart in Figure 4.1, it needed to be turned into a computer program. One important aspect of the computer-assisted scenario-based learning package was the integration of audiovisuals to enhance the realism of the scenario – we did not just want to produce a series of typewritten notes, we wanted to use the multimedia capabilities of the computer. We eventually decided to use stills (photos) rather than video clips, primarily for ready availability, but also to keep the files small. We also had some professionally created audio clips developed to add a further dimension for the students. You will need to carefully consider the copyright of all images and material used, and some of the images we had earlier selected were not included because of doubt about copyright permissions. Inclusion of variations in presentation of material and decisions to be made was essential for maintaining the student's interest and motivation for completing the scenario.

We now knew what we wanted to achieve and how we wanted to achieve it. This gave us a good platform to start looking for appropriate computer programs to develop our SBL scenario. There was a range of software packages available and we finally chose Macromedia Flash and Macromedia Fireworks for implementing the interactive decision-making procedure for the students. It is important to understand that it doesn't matter what package you obtain if you do not get the hard copy right, as no amount of programming will produce a good product.

4. *Testing and evaluation: reflections by our staff and current students*

Once the prototype computer program was developed, our team then reviewed and tested it. Development of the program took much longer than anticipated. This was partly because we had to find someone capable of converting our ideas to the computer and they had to find a suitable software package for converting the material into a computer-assisted program. Our programmer was not local so communication was by email. The program went back and forth among the team quite a few times before Version 1.1 was finally produced. This version was reviewed and tested by one of our teams and also piloted by our students taking the internal Environmental Health Law course.

We asked our internal students to try the interactive program and also complete a questionnaire relating to the program. Sixty per cent of the students in the internal Environmental Health Law paper completed the questionnaire following our trial. The package took an average of 17 minutes to complete and they found the content moderately easy. However, the trial took place at the end of the paper, rather than in the middle, where it will be located in future courses. Overall the students found it well presented and thoroughly enjoyed it. Their responses to the interactive scenario-based learning computer package are shown in Table 4.1.

Table 4.1   Students survey feedback comments

Positive Comments	Criticisms
Good visuals, lets you check your answers at the end	Some ambiguous questions e.g. "how is the order served"
Answering questions	Scrolling too fast (with the form)
Feedback on answers	Too straightforward
Easy to follow	Some lettering too dark on the titles
Good graphics, pictures and quick to operate	Need to identify what you should actually do at the scene
Very realistic	
Helps you to remember details	

Overall the students who tried out this interactive program found it to be a very positive experience and their major suggestion was that all students, not just those in extramural mode, should have access to the case scenario computer package. They were keen for us to develop more scenarios in this paper, and extend the concept into other papers we were responsible for in the Bachelor of Health Science programme.

From here?

The development of this interactive computer program will now allow us to create additional scenario-based learning via the computer. A further aspect we need to develop is to provide for group interaction in the decision-making process. This is important as the group dynamic is necessary for developing professional skills and provides students with the ability to discuss ideas and test out acceptability of their own solutions with their peers. For this scenario we would expect group input once all the data has been presented, but this may be different for other case scenarios. For the extramural mode of delivery we can establish a group dynamic by setting up web-based discussion groups or online chat groups. This could allow the lecturer to become involved in these discussions if necessary. The discussion groups will provide the extramural students with the teacher–student and student–student interactions that are already established for internal students.

Conclusion

We found there was nothing available either commercially or privately and so quite a lot of time and effort went into the production of this first scenario. From our experience with developing and designing the hard copy scenario-based-learning document and the resulting computer program, there were a number of key points essential for its success. These key points are:

- Make the scenario realistic
- Work through the options – consider all the possibilities
- Provide supplementary information as needed
- Include appropriate audio and visuals
- Give the student a variety of feedback types
- Supply examples for comparison
- Develop the scenario before buying the software.

The knowledge gained from developing this first scenario will be used in the development of many more such programs in the future. We believe we can reduce the 18 months this development took to six months or less. We now have the software, the ideas and the expertise to fairly quickly do many more similar case scenarios. These scenarios can be used by internal and extramural students and can be introduced into a range of different media for the student such as online or CD-ROM.

Originally our idea was to use this interactive program for only our extramural students. From the survey results, it seems the internal students would like to have access to this scenario computer package as well.

Overall this computer-assisted scenario-based-learning package has provided an interesting and exciting way of maintaining student interest, and enhancing the decision-making processes for both our internal and extramural students taking the Environmental Health Law paper.

The interactive program will enable students to make decisions based on the material provided but will also deliver alternative solutions showing the best and most cost effective way of carrying out the procedure, and the learning experience and knowledge in this paper will be enhanced by this interactive mode of delivery.

Part Two

Problem-based Scenarios

5

Focus farms: Learning scenarios for dairy cattle medicine

T.J.Parkinson

Introduction

In the education of veterinary undergraduates, case-based medicine is just as much a key facet of their clinical training as it is in medical education. Not only do the details of the case itself present learning challenges and teaching opportunities *per se*, but each case presents the veterinary educator with opportunities for developing learning scenarios that far transcend the intrinsic value of the case. Indeed, the case itself is often just the starting point for the learning, since it often allows for the development of iterative 'what if' scenarios as a means of nurturing students' diagnostic and clinical reasoning skills.

Those of us who teach farm animal medicine need to take the use of clinical material a little further than the management of the individual sick animal, for the agricultural veterinary undergraduate has to understand the links between the health, welfare and productivity of farm animals and farm management systems. Opportunities to create this understanding arise when one regards a whole farm as a 'case'. For, whilst the diagnostic reasoning of classical medical education involves the integration of knowledge about normal structure and function, pathology and microbiology (and other subjects) for an individual sick animal, when the whole farm becomes the 'case', further knowledge (including such disciplines as farming systems, animal husbandry, and agricultural economics) has to be added into the equation.

Because of the importance of its livestock industries to the nation's overall economy (Holmes *et al.*, 2002), veterinary teaching in New Zealand puts a strong emphasis upon farm animal health. Using SBL based upon the whole farm, we encourage veterinary students to understand, diagnose and manage problems of farm animal health and production. Relatively simple sets of farm production data are used to create a focus for a wide-ranging consideration of the problems that they may encounter in farm production systems. By doing so, the value of whole-farm clinical material is expanded greatly beyond what could be achieved by simply observing the management of the case by a clinical teacher. Just as importantly, because students are closely engaged with the clinical scenarios, their learning is active, and generic skills of diagnostic reasoning and problem solving are engendered.

Moreover, our use of farm visits changes as the programme progresses. Early on, visits are used not only to provide context (Knowles *et al.*, 1998) for material transmitted (Ramsden, 1992; Pratt, 1999) in didactic components of the programme but also as a means of transmission of primary information. Whilst such uses of farm visits are undoubtedly valuable in earlier stages of the programme, in its latter stages farm visits are used as scenarios to develop students' understanding of the role of the veterinarian in livestock production. So, in learning to develop a picture of the complex processes that make up an agricultural operation, students go through a diagnostic approach that resembles, yet differs from, the approach that is followed with an individual patient: namely, gathering clinical information by history-taking and observation of the farm's physical, animal and human resources (Oxender and Harrington, 1992).

Of course, we also use farm visits to develop students' skills in advising a farmer about the management of his or her animals. In the development of such skills, students' learning has to shift from the relatively straightforward outcomes of observation and interpretation to a complex process of generation of possible future scenarios, evaluation of the probability of their occurrence, and decision-making based upon best- and worst-case scenarios (or upon maximum- or minimum-likelihood scenarios).

Focus farms: SBL in the real world

About 10 years ago, colleagues in the Department of Veterinary Clinical Science initiated the 'focus farm' scheme as a 'capstone' learning experience for final (fifth) year veterinary students. Small groups of students visit the same farm several times during the year. They are given various exercises to undertake (i.e. a winter feed budget and an analysis of herd reproductive performance) and are encouraged to observe the strengths and weaknesses of the farmer's production system.

1. Winter feed budget

The first visit takes place in the autumn, with the primary objective of devising a winter feeding plan. During the visit students have to get to grips with the constraints upon the management options that are available to the farmer, the feed that is available for the winter, and the farmer's production and personal goals for the farm over the coming year. Thereafter, students use a specially-created spreadsheet (Figure 5.1) using Microsoft® Excel Software to develop a feeding scheme for the herd between the time of their visit to the farm and the start of calving in the spring.

This deceptively simple tool allows students to examine in some detail the effects of their proposed feeding regimes upon a key 'bottom line' variable: the availability of feed at the start of calving. Actually, in practice, much learning occurs beyond the overt objectives of the class. For example, different students may have gathered different bits of information during the visit to the farm, and rarely is there complete agreement about details. Doubt, certainty, give and take, disagreement and eventual agreement characterise the debate that takes place in the class after the visit, as the tutor and students strive to reach a consensus about the farmer's intentions.

Figure 5.1. Microsoft Excel spreadsheet for calculating winter feed budget for a dairy farm

Each of the highlighted areas of the spreadsheet can be manipulated by students, as they try to balance the farmer's various goals with the feed resources he has available for the over-wintering of his cows.

Left-margin annotations:
- Feed quality can be altered
- Stock numbers can be altered
- Milking or dry?
- Estimate winter growth rate and the effect of fertiliser
- Use of conserved feed
- One of the important 'bottom lines'

BASIC FEED BUDGET SPREADSHEET, Copyright Massey University, 2000

CLIENT NAME:	Joe Farmer					
PREPARED BY:	A. Student					

START OF PERIOD:	24-Apr-02		GRASS SILAGE	DM%	22%	
			Pasture equiv.		0.90	
			MAIZE SILAGE	DM%	25%	
			Pasture equiv.		1.10	
INITIAL COVER (kg DM/ha):	2000					
Period length (days):	7					

PERIOD ENDS:	1-May-02	8-May-02	15-May-02	22-May-02	29-May-02	5-Jun-02
EFFECTIVE AREA (ha):	110.0	110.0	110.0	110.0	110.0	110.0
DAILY INTAKE:						
Number of milking cows:	345	275	275	275	0	0
Intake (kg DM/head/day):	15.0	15.0	15.0	15.0	0.0	0.0
Number of dry cows:	10	80	80	80	115	115
Intake (kg DM/head/day):	9.8	9.8	9.8	9.8	9.8	10.9
Number of 2 year old heifers:	0	0	0	0	0	0
Intake (kg DM/head/day):	0.0	0.0	0.0	0.0	0.0	0.0
DEMAND:						
Demand (kg DM/ha/day):	47.9	44.6	44.6	44.6	10.2	11.4
Stocking rate (head/ha):	3.2	3.2	3.2	3.2	1.0	1.0
PASTURE:						
Growth (kg DM/ha/day):	10.0	10.0	20.0	20.0	20.0	20.0
Estimate of pasture wasted	0%	0%	0%	0%	0%	0%
Additional growth from N2	2.5	2.5	2.5	2.5	2.5	2.5
Total growth (kg DM/ha/day):	12.5	12.5	22.5	22.5	22.5	22.5
Difference (kg/DM/ha/day):	-35.4	-32.1	-22.1	-22.1	12.3	11.1
SUPPLEMENTS:						
GRASS SILAGE						
Total kg DM/day:	3105	3105	1555	0	0	0
Estimated waste (%):	10%	10%	10%	0%	0%	0%
Total kg DM/day	2515	2515	1260	0	0	0
MAIZE SILAGE						
Total kg DM/day:	0	0	1000	1000	250	250
Estimated waste (%):	0%	0%	10%	10%	10%	10%
Total kg DM/day	0	0	990	990	248	248
TOTAL SUPPLEMENTS						
(kg DM/ha/day):	23	23	20	9	2	2
	35.4	35.4	43.0	31.5	24.8	24.8
SURPLUS-DEFICIT						
(kg DM/ha/day):	-35.44	-32.13	-22.13	-22.13	12.25	11.10
	-12.57	-9.26	-1.68	-13.13	14.50	13.35
FINAL PREDICTED COVER						
(kg DM/ha):	1912	1847	1835	1744	1845	1939

Tutors aim to facilitate, but not dominate, such discussions, and to progress the debate towards consensus. The students also have to learn to translate the (often contradictory) statements given to them by a farmer into 'hard' data that can be entered into a computer spreadsheet. In doing so, students have to make assumptions and interpret data, drawing heavily upon their own underlying knowledge of animal science to do so. This process is challenging to student and tutor alike; each has to justify to each other how and why we interpret data in one way or another. Indeed, I think that much of the value students derive from the process stems from the tutor's ability to facilitate their interpretation of observations they make on the farm. Hence, the ability of students to accurately record and interpret data, and their ability to articulate the assumptions and decisions they have made in their interpretations of the data, are important components of the assessment of this activity.

Once consensus has been reached, the class determines whether the farmer's proposed winter management regime will allow him or her to achieve the objectives set. The farmer's proposed management is examined, then the students are invited to (a) modify the scenario if it fails to meet the farmer's core objectives and (b) see what would happen if unexpected conditions were to be encountered during the forthcoming winter. Conventional wisdom is generally employed in the former process – usually only small modifications are needed to make the system balance. Also, given that the farmers with whom the students work have long experience of livestock management, the ability of the students to check their calculations against the predictions of the farmer gives a useful 'reality' check on the processes they have gone through and the assumptions they have made.

Students are encouraged to think widely about possibilities that they might have to deal with, if, for example, the winter's climate were to be so severe that pasture growth stopped altogether, or if a source of supplementary feed unexpectedly became available/ unavailable. They are also encouraged to think beyond conventional wisdom in developing solutions to the problems they have generated. In doing so, students not only have to rationalise possible solutions to the problems that they have 'created', but they also have to understand the system thoroughly in order to create credible problems to solve.

Thereafter students have to select from the pool of scenarios that they and their peers have generated, the ones that they believe are most pertinent and write a report and action plan for the farmer based upon their selection. The role of the tutor is partly to keep the scenarios that students create in the realms of reality, but also to ensure that they think of the common scenarios that they are likely to encounter. This process of generation of scenarios is an important component of the exercise; so the range and appropriateness of the scenarios that students choose to include in their report to the farmer are further criteria of its assessment.

This report is sent, verbatim and uncensored, to the farmer, who often provides feedback about the students' ideas. Sometimes this is complimentary, and not infrequently a farmer will model (or modify) his entire winter feeding-management strategy based upon a student's recommendations. Sometimes, however, the feedback is less flattering, and the author hears, in no uncertain terms, the shortcomings of his or her proposals. Whichever occurs, the learning can be profound. But perhaps the greatest learning occurs when, two months later, the students revisit the farm and see what the farmer did, what the weather did and what the outcomes were. Some are chastened to see that their predictions were wrong, some are delighted to see that they were right. All, with suitable input from both farmer and tutor, learn much about the vagaries of pastoral livestock farming.

2.   Herd fertility analysis

The second visit to the focus farm examines the effect of management upon key aspects of dairy cattle health, particularly herd fertility, again using the farm records as the basis of a learning scenario.

Briefly, the farmer provides source data on herd fertility, either directly or via the national database of dairy herd records. The students analyse these data through the use of a commercially available computer program (DairyWin®: Figure 5.2). Learning to use the software is a minor, but necessary, component of the exercise, but its main purpose is to teach students how to identify problems in fertility management and how to provide solutions to such problems for the farmer. This exercise is more akin to classical case-based medicine than is the feed-budgeting exercise, except that, as described above, in treating a whole farm as the 'case' students have to integrate knowledge from many areas of the curriculum. In using this exercise as a scenario for developing diagnostic and problem-solving skills, I find that there are some interesting challenges in tutoring the class. Students have to be encouraged to think about what parameters to examine, how to interpret data and so forth; also to understand problems inherent in the data they are using, such as how spurious information can be misleading.

The real challenge for me is to allow students to work out the solutions to the herd's problems for themselves, rather than simply tell them what to do. To solve the problems that are presented to them, students typically have to integrate their knowledge of reproductive physiology, microbiology, epidemiology, pharmacology, animal behaviour, farm management and nutrition; a process that works best when I act as a catalyst for thought rather than as the one who transmits yet more 'information', adding to the curricular overload that so bedevils veterinary education (Cardinet *et al.* 1992; Rex, 1993).

As with the feed budget exercise, the 'reality' of this exercise is enhanced by students' having to report their findings to the farmer. In this case the visit to the farm is made *after* the students have examined the records, so that they will have made initial deductions and come to initial solutions to problems, but will not yet have translated these into a final report. Discussing their views with the farmer during the farm visit means that they get some very direct feedback on their clinical acumen (and, sometimes, on their (lack of) people-handling skills!) Again, students are encouraged to think beyond the conventional wisdom of reproductive management, but, whatever their recommendations, the students are expected to create a report that is professional in its presentation and fully justified in terms of the conclusions that it reaches.

Figure 5.2. Basic DairyWin © output from the analysis of fertility records of a dairy farm

Students identify areas of concern (#) then use further parts of the programme to identify causes/reasons for the problems they have noted. Subsequently, students have to devise solutions to these problems and present them to the farmer in a justified report.

Reproductive Monitor Report Stock Class: Adult Cow	Period 1	Target
CALVING PERFORMANCE		
4-Week Calving Rate	68%	67%
8-Week Calving Rate	91%	95%
SUBMISSION RATES		
Percent Calved <40 days at PSM	20%	10%
21 Day Submission Rate	60%	90%
28 Day Submission Rate	71%	92%
RETURN INTERVALS		#
Return Intervals %2–17 days	20%	13%
Return Intervals %18–24 days	56%	69%
Return Intervals %39–45 days	11%	7%
CONCEPTION RATES		#
1st Service 49 Day NR	44%	61%
Total Service 49 Day NR	51%	61%
1ST Service Pregnancy Rate	42%	60%
Total Service Pregnancy Rate	39%	60%
Services per Conception	2.6	1.7
IN CALF RATES		#
4-week In-Calf Rate	49%	57%
8-week In-Calf Rate	70%	86%
% Not In Calf by PSM + 165 days	18%	7%

Learning outcomes

The learning outcomes that I seek to achieve from using focus farms as learning scenarios are:

1) providing a bridge for the translation of animal science and clinical medicine theory into a 'real life' practical situation

2) gathering accurate data (i.e. the generic skill of taking a clinical history) and developing group consensus (i.e. the generic skill of team-work)

3) developing diagnostic and clinical reasoning skills, in a context that is markedly different from most of the rest of the veterinary degree programme (which is primarily concerned with problems of individual sick animals)

4) developing feasible scenarios of farm management (i.e. because one must have a deep understanding of how a system works before one can manipulate it)

5) solving farm management problems (in which problem solving is developed as a generic skill, but in the specific context of farm animal medicine)

6) providing feedback from the client: students receive the farmers' personal critique of their ideas. I think that this is a crucial aspect of the learning; for, as a result, a learning experience which could easily be regarded by the students as a hypothetical 'exercise' is placed into the 'real' world: it is by no means uncommon for a farmer to implement the recommendations that were made by an insightful student.

The use of focus farms, mid-way between a 'teaching exercise' and a 'clinical case', seems to be a useful method of facilitating learning at the interface between farm animal medicine and production. Students are actively involved in the evaluation, diagnosis and solving of problems that they encounter on the farms, so the learning which they attain is far deeper than if they were simply to observe an experienced clinician going through the problem-solving process. As others have previously reported, involvement in (rather than observation of) production medicine investigations heightens students' engagement in the activity, resulting in deeper learning (e.g. Sprecher and Farmer, 1994; Singer and Hardin, 1997; Regula et al., 1999). I think that much of the strength of these activities is that they meet students' need to be provided with 'a "real-world" problem situation [since] if the problem is too narrow or constrained it loses its authenticity' (Singer and Hardin, p.8).

Conclusions

For the tutor, SBL provides an opportunity to explore students' understanding of farm animal management systems and medicine *per se*, plus the interrelationships between the two. Discussion in tutorials invariably throws students' questions back upon their own resources of basic and clinical scientific knowledge, with the aim of stimulating the process of integration that is needed to solve problems highlighted by the scenarios.

Perhaps the fact that students can try out ideas without having to live with the consequences of being wrong is part of the strength of these focus farm visits. Also, since the outcomes of their thinking are also presented to the farmer, students probably take far more care over their problem-solving and reporting processes than if their work was only assessed by university staff. Whilst the feedback is not as immediate as can be achieved through exercises that are undertaken completely online (Papa et al., 1999), the need for relevant, critical feedback is nonetheless met. Thus, the final (summative) assessment and, probably more importantly, the comments that the students receive from the farmers provide them with feedback that is valid in terms of their academic achievement and in terms of the likely acceptability of their advice to future farming clients.

Finally, the use of SBL in the context of farm visits/farm animal medicine directs students' learning away from the memorisation of details to the interpretation of observations through the synthesis of principles derived from a wide range of knowledge. In terms of Biggs' (1999:37) Structure of the Observed Learning Outcome (SOLO) taxonomy, the purpose is to achieve learning outcomes which are ideally at the 'extended abstract' level and certainly are at the 'relational' level. Ideally, developing such integrative behaviour is a generic skill that should be of use to students in a wide range of clinical situations; although, in fact, some students go through the process in a mechanical way, or limit the learning into the specific area of dairy cattle management and fail to transfer its principles into a generic skill. For those whose interests lie with farm animals feed budgeting and fertility analysis [is] good. Dealing with a real case helps maintain interest and is definitely realistic.

Acknowledgements

The Focus Farm scheme was devised and introduced by N.B. Williamson during the 1980s. I am grateful to M. Stevenson (Institute of Veterinary Animal and Biological Sciences, Massey University) for permission to reproduce part of the feed budget spreadsheet and to the Livestock Improvement Corporation for permission to reproduce DairyWin® output.

References

Biggs, J. (1999), *Teaching for quality learning at university,* Society for Research in Higher Education, Buckingham: Open University Press.

Cardinet, G.H., Gourley, I.M., BonDurant, R.H. *et al.* (1992), 'Changing dimensions of veterinary medical education in pursuit of diversity and flexibility in service to society', *Journal of the American Veterinary Medical Association*, no.201, pp.1530–1539.

Holmes, C.W., Wilson, G.F., MacKenzie, D.D., Brookes, I.M., Parkinson, T.J. and Garrick, D. (2002), *Milk production from pasture* (2nd ed.), Palmerston North: Massey Printery.

Knowles, M.S., Holton E.F. and Swanson R.A. (1998), *The adult learner*, Houston, Texas: Gulf Publishing.

Oxender, W.D. and Harrington, B.D. (1992), 'Integrating production medicine and large animal production into the veterinary curriculum for students to create an active learning program', *Journal of the American Veterinary Medical Association*, no.201, pp.1358–1362.

Papa, F.J., Aldrich, D. and Schumacker, R.E. (1999), 'The effects of immediate online feedback upon diagnostic performance', *Academic Medicine*, no.74 (Oct. suppl.), S16–S18.

Pratt, D.D. (1999), *Five perspectives on teaching in adult and higher education,* Florida, USA: Kreiger Publishing Co.

Ramsden, P. (1992), *Learning to teach in higher education*, London: Routledge

Regula, G., Heuwieser, W., Hallmann, T. and Schimmelpfennig, K. (1999), 'Teaching bovine reproduction with the computer: a comparison between a tutorial and a case-based approach', *Journal of Veterinary Medical Education*, no. 26, pp.10–15.

Rex, M. (1993), 'Veterinary education in the world: Changing attitudes', *Australian Veterinary Journal*, no.70B, pp.369–372.

Singer, J. and Hardin, L. (1997), 'Educational perspectives of teaching ruminant nutritional management in a problem-based elective course', *Journal of Veterinary Medical Education*, no. 24, pp.5–9.

Sprecher, D.J. and Farmer, J.A. (1994), 'Having students as integral rather than peripheral participants in production medicine investigations', *Journal of Veterinary Medical Education*, no.21, pp.47–50.

6

Giving a context to learning

Errol Thompson

Introduction

Can a scenario be used as the base for a programme of learning in a subject area? Roger Schank (1992) argues that it can. In this chapter, I describe how I use a scenario as the structuring tool for a paper in computer software development. The learning outcomes in these papers involve developing skills in: using development tools such as design tools or programming languages, understanding process issues; and evaluating different approaches and solutions. I place an emphasis on the development of reflective practitioners and critical thinkers within the discipline. With my scenario, I endeavour to provide a real-world environment for the learning and development of these skills. In this chapter I describe the way I structure the paper and my experience in teaching using this approach. I discuss the problems and possibilities to reveal avenues for further exploration.

Early in my teaching career, I became frustrated that students in their assignments would submit back definitions and content of a paper with minimal reflection. Requested evaluations would do little more than compare features or process steps. Their assignments would show that they had no understanding of how the material being learnt might relate to software development in the 'real world'; nor could they see that an evaluation might have relevance in a business context. As I reviewed the students' work against the assessment criteria, I wondered whether there was a better way to write the assignments that would cause students to address the issues in a business context.

My solution to this assessment problem was to attempt to write my assignment briefs so that they described a business scenario in which the skill or knowledge that I was assessing needed to be applied. I would introduce a manager who would then describe the required systems development task that he wanted completed. The output of the assessment was to be a business report or part of a small business application. Where I wanted them to address what might have been considered academic issues, I endeavoured to write the scenario so that they had to defend a point of view to the manager and support that point of view with appropriate references to academic resources.

Using scenarios in assessment raised additional issues that students claimed were not covered in the lectures or course materials. My lectures often gave students material without context or presented the material followed by a brief scenario as an illustration of the application of the context. I was forced to look at my teaching method so that I was providing context for the material that I was teaching.

Within the teaching environment of the institution, the focus was on utilising problem-based learning. However, the problems would often be a sequence of exercises with little relationship to each other, other than the technique or skill that the student was expected to utilise. Would it be possible to develop a business scenario from which a sequence of problems could be developed? I am now looking at how to extend the use of a scenario to drive the direction of the lectures, tutorials and self-paced learning exercises. The scenario that I am developing is based on the following:

Competitive Cycles Corporation is a manufacturer of road racing and competitive mountain bicycles. Since their founding, they have used manual administrative and management systems. Now, as they look at international expansion of their business, they want to move to computerised systems. You are being asked to ...

Paper structure

If we start with the above scenario framework, how should the paper be structured? The paper structure presented here is based primarily on the design used for distance learning (Thompson, 1997). The structure was developed as a result of the way that I wrote my assessments and not because of any desire to use scenario-based learning. The realisation that we[1] were using a scenario-based learning approach came much later when I was investigating different approaches to developing an online learning environment. Figure 6.1 endeavours to depict the structure that I used. The following discussion endeavours to describe the component parts and to present the reasoning.

Welcome to the paper

In the structuring of the papers, we wanted to draw the students into a business context that would simulate the type of business environment in which the skills they were learning would be used. The first thing we wanted the students to read was a letter of appointment to a role within the organisation. In a paper focused on systems design and development, the letter welcomed them in as trainee programmers or system designers. Since this was a distance learning paper, we also included a paper overview

---

[1]   In the institution that I was working in, the writer of the distance-learning materials worked closely with an instructional designer and other writing project team members. The initial structure was proposed by the instructional designer and revised by the team as I wrote the resources. I use 'we' in this paper to refer to decisions made by the team.

Figure 6.1 Paper structure

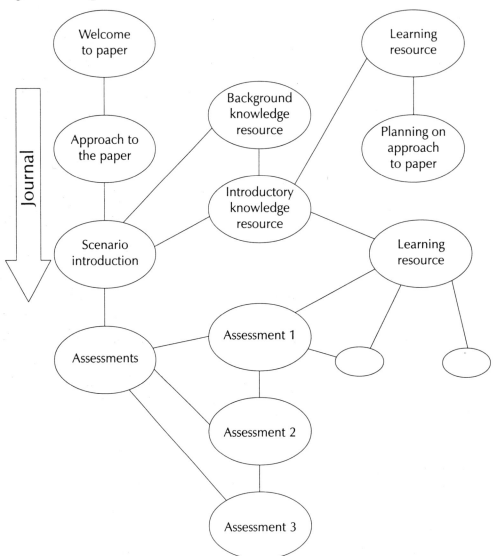

that included administrative details, information about lecturers, how to access library resources, how to use the mailing list, and how to use the audio-conference facilities.

Approach to the paper

This element was not included in our original materials. I added it after many students said that they didn't understand how to approach the paper and the sequence in which to study the resources. In this section, I suggested the approach a student should take when attempting to complete the paper. I used the same style and structure as the learning resources so the student would also gain experience in working with the resources.

Scenario introduction

Following the letter, we included material to introduce the scenario. This set of material included background about the organisation, its philosophy and its expectations of its employees. This material focused on helping students understand the organisation and their role within the organisation. It also covered prerequisite knowledge and planning issues. The aim of the welcome and scenario introduction was to set the tone for the paper and to provide an overview of the direction the paper and assignments would take. To support the rational introducing the scenario, I wrote a number of learning resources the students could use if they felt that they lacked the prerequisite knowledge or wanted more guidance on preparing a plan for completing the paper.

Assignments

Following the welcome material, we placed the assignments or projects that the student would have to complete. I wrote these as an extension of the scenario introduction in the form of mini-projects being assigned to the new employee. In the systems design and development paper, they included part of a system design for which the students were given an analysis document and a programming exercise. These assignments were selected for their fit with the learning outcomes for the paper and would define the direction for study within the paper, with each assignment providing a number of learning goals for a block of study.

Journal

As part of the assessment strategy, students completed a journal. This was introduced to the papers as a way of fostering some of the higher cognitive skills and in particular critical thinking (November 1996; November 1997). I was conscious that in a distance-learning mode, it was not possible to observe the students as they worked on the tasks raised by the scenarios. I hoped that their journal would give me insight into the approach that they took and their personal experience in wrestling with the subject matter. The journal would also foster learning reinforcement through the telling of stories (Schank, 1990).

Learning resources

Since the assignments were mini-projects, I used a project plan to determine the tasks that needed to be completed for the assessment scenarios. For each task, I wrote a learning resource based on a task-specific mini-scenario (i.e. you have been asked to prepare a data-flow diagram for this process). If students could complete the task described in the mini-scenario to the defined criteria (included in the learning resource following the mini-scenario), they did not need to complete the learning resource. The main body of the learning resource was a set of hierarchical problems and associated reference resources that built the knowledge and skills required to complete the mini-scenario. These were structured so that each problem was progressively harder and built on the knowledge or skill set developed in previous exercises.

Map of learning resources

To aid students in developing a strategy for completing the paper, I included a map of the learning resources with the introductory materials that presented the possible sequencing or dependencies between these resources. My underlying philosophy was that students would examine the scenario and the assessments and then evaluate what learning resources they needed to complete. An underlying goal was to have the students develop a reflective (Schön, 1983) and experiential approach (Boud, 1993; Kolb, 1984) to their learning. I endeavoured to ensure that there was no enforced sequence to completing of learning resources and that students were not compelled to complete any of the learning resources if they could already complete the assignments. This model is similar to the case-based teaching architecture that promotes the "idea that learning takes place on a need-to-know basis" (Schank and Jona, 1990: 8).

Classroom context issues

In moving to the classroom context, I wanted to use the same resources and paper structure. To achieve this, I am structuring lectures around completing a mini-scenario, similar to that used in a learning resource, that I expect the students to complete. I endeavour to illustrate the process and the reasoning for a given solution. Having presented the mini-scenario, I then work through the scenario issues using a series of questions that relate to the required learning and progress to achieving the scenario outcome. At times through the session, I endeavour to encourage the students to add their input. At this point in my use of scenarios in lectures, I have been selecting the learning resources and mini-scenarios to be used but I see a possibility that for a given lecture session, these might be decided based on questions raised by students as they work through the assessment and learning tasks.

For tutorial sessions, I allow the students to raise any questions related to the paper. In some ways, I would like to see these dominate the tutorial sessions. However, I find few students come prepared with questions, so I direct the students to a specific learning resource and its mini-scenario. Because we have different tutors taking these sessions, in the lecture session following a tutorial session, I am endeavouring to present the main outcomes from the tutorial as a form of feedback.

Teaching experience

In systems development, the topics are clearly related as part of a process in which the developer increases their understanding of the requirements for a system and translates the requirements into the design of one, and ultimately to the implementation of an operational system. Often in the process, the developer has to make decisions about the different tools or techniques that are appropriate to utilise. With the learning scenarios that we wrote, we reflected the project nature of this environment, endeavouring to follow the normal sequence of a project.

As an approach for structuring a set of scenarios, this seemed quite logical and follows the sequence in systems analysis and design textbooks. This sequence is effective where students already have an understanding of the expected final outcomes and want to learn the tools and techniques. However, students who have little experience of business systems and even less experience of computer systems are lost and confused until very late in the process, when they finally see the results coming together. As I write this paper, I am investigating learning-in-doing (Lave and Wenger, 1991; McBreen, 2001; Wenger, 1998), where apprenticeship models are discussed. In this context, apprentices start on the peripheral tasks – often the finishing tasks (i.e. writing a function) – and as their skill set develops are introduced to the more central tasks (i.e. analysis and design) and finally the process as a whole. Some learning in this model is achieved simply by being a participant and observer of the process.

I am now reviewing my scenario-based approach. Structurally, the paper will remain unchanged (i.e. I will still use the structure presented in Figure 6.1). Students will still be introduced to the organisation and the assignments but the initial assignment scenarios will engage the students in a series of peripheral, apprentice-type tasks that will build an understanding of the end result and the skills needed to achieve these end outputs. For example, with an object-oriented design and development paper, the students will be given a scenario that requires them to analyse the behaviour of an object from the code for the object's class. Later, they will look at the interaction between classes and how these can be described using the modelling tools. The final scenario and assessment will involve developing an object-oriented design for a small system.

With the assignment scenarios that I currently use, students show confusion with respect to what they are supposed to do, and seek additional help to find their way into the scenarios. Being given options and choices is not a familiar educational experience. These students give the impression of wanting more structure and direction; they did not see the map of the path through the learning resources as a guide and sought defined learning targets for each week based on the selection of specific learning resources.

In the distance-learning context, I used audio conferences with defined topics and mailing list discussions as a way of helping these students develop a direction through the materials. Schank (1990) discusses the use of "What next" buttons in learning environments so that students can gain additional guidance to overcome these difficulties. My revised approach with smaller, more focused initial assignment scenarios should also address this issue. However, there always need to be resources that will give additional guidance to the students.

In the classroom and university context, I have found it more difficult to introduce a scenario approach. In part this is because I initially did not have the set of learning resources to support student learning. As my learning resources have been developed and improved, it has become easier. However, there are still difficulties.

In the distance-learning context, not all students need to be following the same path through the scenarios. Most students work independently of any other student except possibly for interactions in the mailing list or audio conferences. This means that they do not travel at the same pace. Allowing for different paths or pace is more difficult to manage when there is a weekly scheduled lecture and large class sizes. Time isn't available for the lecturer to work with individuals, and lectures are often scheduled to deal with specific topics on given days. This does not stop a scenario being used as the base for the teaching but it does force students to be more in step in their learning and the environment to be more directed. With smaller classes, a more flexible approach is possible.

I am investigating making the lectures and tutorials more flexible in terms of scenarios. I am looking at a session structure that might:

1. review the set self-study scenario and issues from associated readings, possibly using self- or peer-assessment
2. deliver a twenty-minute lecture springboard scenario (Denning, 2001) for the next set of mini-scenarios to be considered (the exact springboard scenario may be selected from a range depending on the outcome of a previous exercise or some other feedback)
3. complete a set of mini-scenarios in groups to reinforce/build on the lecture springboard scenario
4. complete a formative assessment that reviews and seeks to uncover the direction for the next session (again this could be self- or peer-assessed during the session and collected in)
5. outline readings for the next session and self-study scenarios.

I see it as important for the number of lecture storyboard scenarios and self-study scenario sets to exceed the available sessions so that a choice of path can be made. If the number of storyboard scenarios available were merely equal to the number of lecture slots planned, there would be minimal flexibility in the direction in which the paper could go during the teaching semester. Regardless of the teaching path, I would endeavour to make all assessments and learning resources available to students at the beginning of the semester. The goal in the lecture session would be to provide feedback, to provide direction, and to stimulate engagement with the subject.

Students in a classroom setting appear to be less willing to work through learning resources. They have an expectation that the lecturer will direct them as to what to do next and will tell them all that they need to know and do, even if this knowledge and direction is obtained from the scenarios and supporting learning resources. This was shown in a recent semester when students were asked to indicate what learning resources they had used outside the classroom and tutorial sessions. The majority of students had not completed any additional exercises. Some went further and complained that because I had not covered some topics directly in a class session, they had not been taught that material – even though this material was covered in the scenarios and learning resources. In some cases, they had been explicitly told to read or complete exercises on the topic. This may be an indication that the students are not engaging with the materials or that they are having trouble determining the direction. The revised lecture and tutorial approach may address some of these issues.

Another problem that I am wrestling with is the role of the textbook in scenario-based learning. In information systems development, textbooks do work through the systems development process, often using a scenario to illustrate the points raised in the text. The scenario is not used to drive the learning. It is a resource to show the results of applying the process or technique. I see the role of a textbook in scenario-based learning as that of the primary reference material. The student should be able to use it to locate information related to the technical detail or rules for the task. In the systems development context, it might provide the rules for a particular diagramming technique or describe an approach to using a particular technique.

As I review the sequence of my scenarios, I am aware that the sequence in which a textbook deals with topics will be in the reverse order to that in which I want to raise the issues. The exception may be some texts that teach programming languages. As a result, I am now looking for reading resources that I can easily link with individual mini-scenarios. The nature of these reading resources will also change, as they need to focus on technical details or stimulate thinking on the issues raised by the scenario.

The risks

Scenario-based learning, if implemented fully, passes control of learning to the student and can liberate students to pursue paths in which they are interested rather than the defined learning outcomes of a programme (Schank and Jona, 1990). This could lead to a possibility that the paper is not delivering the anticipated outcomes especially if those outcomes are defined in terms of a specific set of knowledge requirements. Schank (2001) sees this as one of the inhibitors for the revolutionising of teaching using innovative learning technologies.

I have endeavoured to avoid this problem by controlling the range of learning resources made available. However, I have also provided students with opportunities to explore areas of personal interest, as long as those areas fit within or are close to the intended learning outcomes for the paper.

The greatest risk is to leave students confused by the scenario and unsure of what they are attempting to achieve. It is important that the scenario is introduced in a context that fosters exploration of the problem space and encourages students to develop this exploration. The initial presentation of the scenario will either inspire learning or leave the students confused and unsure where to begin. It is important that the students are inspired. I would like to say there is a simple formula for achieving this, but so far I haven't found it.

A lower risk is to fail to provide all the learning resources that students might need. Some would argue that this is an indication of poor planning. A scenario throws up different problems for different learners. It isn't like preparing a fixed sequence of lectures or learning resources to be studied in a fixed sequence. When scenario-based learning is used with a lecture-based paper, additional topics can be covered by new lectures. In a distance-learning environment, it is more difficult to prepare and make available additional learning resources. Some online learning environments can make new learning resources available more easily.

I am wary of rushing to prepare new resources. I endeavour to determine the importance of the topic to the paper and whether there are alternative ways for the students to obtain the required knowledge. If a topic is taking a student down a side path that could be dealt with outside the paper, I indicate that to the student. Where students can learn the additional topic through readings or by carrying out their own research, I point them to some of those resources.

Conclusion

In developing the paper structure described, I developed an overriding scenario that gave a context to the learning. This overriding scenario provided an open-ended problem environment. The same scenario with minor modifications has been used in a range of papers in Information Systems. The assessment scenarios are more structured and provide the primary focal direction for the learning. These scenarios are still open in the sense that there is a range of problems that the student needs to resolve. Some will not be central to the learning of the paper. The most focused are the mini-scenarios included in the learning resources. I focus these scenarios on a specific skill or knowledge segment.

This structure has been used in paper-based distance-learning and lecture environments. It is an effective structure for the self-paced study of the distance-learning environment. However, translation to the in-step nature of the lecture and tutorial environment has proved more difficult. Tailoring is continuing.

References

Boud, D. (1993), 'Experience as the base for learning', *Higher Education Research and Development*, vol.12, no.1, pp.33–44.

Denning, S. (2001), *The springboard: How storytelling ignites action in knowledge-era organizations*, Boston: Butterworth-Heinemann.

Kolb, D.A. (1984), *Experiential learning: Experience as the source of learning and development*, Englewood Cliffs: Prentice Hall.

Lave, J. and Wenger, E. (1991), *Situated learning: Legitimate peripheral participation*, Cambridge, UK: Cambridge University Press.

McBreen, P. (2001), *Software craftsmanship: The new imperative*, Boston: Addison-Wesley.

November, P. (1996), 'Journals for the journey into deep learning: A framework', *Higher Education Research and Development*, vol.15, no.1, pp.115–127.

November, P. (1997), 'Learning to teach experientially: A pilgrim's progress', *Studies in Higher Education*, vol.22, no.3, pp.289–299.

Schank, R.C. (1990), *Tell me a story: Narrative and intelligence*, Evanston, IL: Northwestern University Press.

Schank, R.C. (1992) *Goal-based scenarios*, Technical Report 36, Evanston, IL: Northwestern University.

Schank, R.C. (2001), 'Revolutionizing the traditional classroom course', *Communications of the ACM*, vol.44, no.12, pp.21–24.

Schank, R.C. and Jona, M.Y. (1990), *Empowering the student: New perspectives on the design of teaching systems*. Technical Report 4, Evanston, IL: Northwestern University.

Schön, D.A. (1983), *The reflective practitioner: How professionals think in action*, New York: Basic Books.

Thompson, E. (1997), *71253 Systems Design and Development*, Lower Hutt: The Open Polytechnic of New Zealand.

Wenger, E. (1998), *Communities of practice: Learning, meaning and identity*, Cambridge, UK: Cambridge University Press.

7

Essential slices of reality: Constructing problem-based scenarios that work

T.M.Stewart

Introduction

Life, both personal and professional, is a series of challenges. Problems abound everywhere we look! In all spheres of life we are constantly required to apply analytical and decision-making skills to problematic situations.

How can we teach these skills in the classroom environment? A problem-based learning (PBL) approach is an effective way of achieving this goal (Savery and Duffy, 1995; Shank, 1996). PBL provides a constructivist learning environment rather than an instructivist one. One manifestation of this approach is to present a real-world task or problem to students (a problem-based scenario), which they then must work through step by step.

In this chapter, I will share my experiences as a teacher who has used problem-based scenarios to facilitate learning, and offer some rules on "the art" of developing and using such scenarios.

How problem-based scenarios solved a teaching problem

Pest and disease diagnosis is an important skill every potential crop consultant needs to acquire. Within my plant pathology course I lecture on the deductive process required for this task. These lectures used to be complemented by laboratory classes where students were required to seek out pest and disease-ridden specimens somewhere in their local environment (their gardens, the university grounds, local parks etc.) and bring them into the laboratory. Once there, they set about trying to diagnose what the problem might be, identifying insects or any other creatures found on the plants, or isolating suspected pathogens.

Whilst the lab exercises gave students experience in identifying pests and above ground pathogens, they really only provided a subset of the whole diagnostic process. They were inadequate training for diagnosing other, less obvious, causes of an unhealthy crop. Those conditions needed to be investigated more deeply, and such investigation requires not only field research, but also research into the history of the crop, past weather conditions and a host of other mitigating and predisposing factors.

While pondering how these concepts could be brought home to students, it occurred to me that what was needed was some kind of controlled scenario, where students were actually presented with a sick crop and could be given the opportunity to explore the situation within a given set of circumstances (i.e. scenario parameters). This would be an exercise that reflected the reality of what students could expect after they graduated and started work as crop consultants. The difference was that here they would be able to make incorrect diagnoses and provide recommendations that were clearly wrong without the risk of a lawsuit. Also, they could be provided with feedback, which showed them where they went wrong and suggested how an expert would have tackled this case. In essence, the students could make mistakes and learn from them.

To give students this experience a virtual reality computer-based "simulation" was developed, called DIAGNOSIS, which presented these scenarios to students (Stewart *et al.*, 2001; Stewart, 2002). Those wishing to view this on screen may visit us at *http://www.diagnosis.co.nz*

DIAGNOSIS has now evolved into a generic problem-based scenario-authoring tool called CHALLENGE (Stewart, 2002). CHALLENGE allows problem-based scenarios to be authored in any domain. CHALLENGE can be viewed at: *http://challenge.massey.ac.nz*

How to construct problem-based scenarios in any domain

What follows are the steps I took to construct problem-based scenarios in my own teaching which can be applied to almost any learning domain. However, do note that such scenarios are not restricted to a CHALLENGE exercise. In fact, no software at all is needed to present problem-based scenarios. A teacher with a whiteboard or with images or slides can present the observations to students during a tutorial. If a "guided approach" is needed, the students can be stepped through as they go. Scenarios can also be outlined completely on paper, although these are less interactive. So here are the steps:

Step 1 – Define the learning objectives

When using problem-based scenarios it is important to have a clear idea of why they are being used. For instance, are they being used to assess students on how well they have absorbed the facts, processes and methodologies that may have been provided from lectures, books or similar passive activities? On the other hand, problem-based scenarios could be used for acquiring such knowledge in the first instance, by making them central to the course. Students could work through increasingly complex scenarios, receiving expert feedback at every step. This is the "goal-based" scenario approach favoured by some authors (Shank, 1996).

I use the former approach with my own students. I tend to create a "subset of reality" with places, objects and people that tend to exist in the real-world environment and that, in a diagnostic scenario, might *potentially* need to be examined or investigated to confirm or reject a particular hypothesis. For example, in a typical orchard situation there might be a grower, the affected trees themselves (with all their plant parts), a sprayer, a fertiliser applicator, soil, weeds, insect traps and possibly even the spray field representative and the neighbour. In the laboratory, I might provide a selected number of common diagnostic tests. Any *one* scenario would not require the student to interact with *all* these objects or people, but they generally are provided, nevertheless.

The learning objective of this approach is more one of a test. While they may have to look up specific facts, students should already have some foundation knowledge (or at least know where to look for it) that the scenario induces them to use. Subsequently, students are graded on their performance and this grade often counts towards their final assessment for the plant pathology course.

Other teachers, however, including some who have used CHALLENGE, prefer a more guided approach. At every stage of the assessment, hypotheses are offered, students select possibilities and then are given the correct answers with reasons as to why they are correct. Here, scenarios are used to acquire domain knowledge at each step. How students perform in the scenario process may be less important than what they have gained by simply going through the process. After all, we do learn from our mistakes.

Sometimes a scenario may be used solely for discussion. For example, in developing CHALLENGE we constructed a scenario for schoolchildren where they could investigate why fish kept dying in a particular household. The reason was that the fishbowl was filled up with water from the swimming pool and the high levels of chlorine killed the fish. Children discover this as they work through the scenario. The exercise can be used to introduce students to the hazards of household chemicals.

When formulating the learning objectives it is also worth considering how much time students will be given to work through a scenario. Will it be hours, days or weeks? If students are required to look up information in order to successfully complete the scenario, this will take time. How much time should be given for student reflection? For my own students, I normally allow three hours per exercise. This, in my opinion, is enough time to complete the observations and tests, absorb the results, look up any information they need and compile a short report. It would be the same amount of "thinking time" a consultant might spend on a problem of this nature.

Step 2 – Decide on a scenario

Coming up with a good scenario is not always easy. First, think of the learning objectives of the exercise, then think of a real-world problem that relates to these learning objectives. Some guidelines are:

- Ensure the problem will challenge the student, yet be solvable at his or her level. Normally, it should be sufficiently complex so that the solution is not obvious to the user when presented with the initial scenario information. On the other hand, scenarios must not be so difficult that the student gets frustrated, or gives up.

- Enlist the help of experts if needed. If possible the exercise should be constructed by, or with the aid of, people who have actually "been there and done that". In other words, they should reflect a real-life situation in which the domain expert has participated.

- Consider using existing reports. Even if you have not experienced the scenario first-hand, you may be able to engineer one from a report written by someone who has. Students can be given the raw data from the report to undertake their own analysis. The report is essentially the model answer. Of course if a scenario is prepared this way, the original writers of the report should be acknowledged.

- Adapt an existing problem-solving exercise. Examples of problem-based scenarios can be found scattered throughout the Web and in literature. These may simply need adapting to your own circumstances.

Step 3 – Determine how the scenario will be presented

In what ways will students be interacting with this scenario? Will it be presented and discussed in a tutorial, outlined in text and pictures as a Web-or paper-based exercise or presented using a specific software package such as CHALLENGE? Will it be tackled by individual students, students in pairs, small groups, or the whole class? Personally, I have found pairs to work well.

The resources available and the learning objectives will influence how the scenario will be presented. For example, a tutorial step-through of a scenario with discussion may not be appropriate where an assessment of competency is required.

Step 4 – Determine the objects and tasks that are essential for the correct hypothesis to be proven

One of the first things to do is to define the approach an experienced practitioner would take to solving the problem. In order to pursue and confirm the correct hypothesis, what observations would they make, and in what order (if any)? What tests would they use? These will form your "must-have" observations, procedures and tests for the scenario. How much do the results of these tasks contribute to the correct answer? Some will be contributing and some will be definitive. Decide how observations pointing to the correct solution (i.e. reinforcing the correct hypothesis) will be presented and where.

For example, consider a plant diagnostic problem where the cause is a particular root-rotting fungus, say *Phytophthora cactorum* (Table 7.1). The following table was prepared for my own use, when developing the scenario for the CHALLENGE program. However, this kind of table is helpful for developing any problem-based scenario, where the cause of a problem needs to be determined. It shows observations that will lead the student to a realisation that this fungus is indeed the culprit. By the time they are ready to take samples to the laboratory, *Phytophthora cactorum* should be high on the list of suspects. In the lab, they can then choose the correct tests to reveal this pathogen. Students will only uncover the *observations* in the course of their investigation (in my case, these observations are presented by the CHALLENGE program). It will be up to them to decide on the significance and overall weight of evidence.

Table 7.1   Key observations, their significance and their contributions towards accepting the hypothesis that *Phytophthora cactorum* is indeed the major problem affecting this crop

Observation	Significance	Contribution towards weight of evidence that *Phytophthora cactorum* is the causal agent of the disease
In the Field		
All leaves are yellowing and branches are showing die-back on affected trees.	Classic symptoms of a root problem	Contributing. Many organisms can affect the roots of trees.
Worst affected plants, in the low lying areas.	Fungal root rots are often dependent on high moisture levels in the soil.	Contributing
Drainage is poor.	Fungal root rots are often dependent on high moisture levels in the soil.	Contributing
Weeds present are indicative of a wet soil	Fungal root rots are often dependent on high moisture levels in the soil.	Contributing
Fruit Variety is Cox's Orange Pippin. Other varieties seem ok.	An older apple variety known to be have high susceptibility to this pathogen.	Strong contributor
Trees show a canker (diseased sunken area) at the base of the tree, if the bark is cut away.	*Phytophthora cactorum* often forms a canker (diseased sunken area) at the base.	Major Clue. Only a few fungal pathogens cause this symptom and *Phytophthora cactorum* is one of them.
There is no sign of fungal fruiting bodies or fan-shaped fungal growth under the bark over the diseased area.	White root rot caused by *Armallaria mellea* can cause a similar canker but the fungal structures described to the left are almost always present. Disease is probably not caused by *A. mellea*.	Contributor by practically eliminating one of the alternative possible causes
In the Laboratory		
Foot and root samples tested for *P. cactorum*	Trees are infected with *Phytophthroa cactorum*.	Definitive

All these tasks and observations need to be available in the scenario so that students can confirm what they initially might suspect.

Of course, knowing what is infecting the plant is one thing. Why such a thing happened and what to do about it is another. This is also a required part of the scenario analysis and students should be required to include the cause of the problem and their recommended solution(s) in their report. That being the case, recommendations as to what should be done about the identified problem need to be decided on by the tutor for the debriefing or discussion at the end. In the case above, improved drainage and more tolerant varieties are the answer.

Step 5 – Add observations and tasks that allow alternative hypotheses to be explored

As a student works through a problem-based scenario, he or she will form hypotheses, from which lines of enquiry will develop to prove or disprove them. In real-life situations things are often not clear-cut. There may be many possibilities, and initially some hypotheses may seem quite valid which on further investigation prove to be wrong.

It is important that scenarios contain scope for investigating these alternatives. Consequently they should have a fair share of misleading observations or "red-herrings". These are very useful for teaching students to be thorough in their analysis, and not to jump to early conclusions, especially if they are the kinds of red herrings which occur in real life.

Again, to use our root rot example, several alternative lines of inquiry have been included. One involves the weeds in the orchard. If the student examines the weeds closely, they appear to be affected by something. A (valid) hypothesis may arise in the mind of the student that whatever is affecting the weeds is also affecting the tree – a weedkiller, perhaps? In asking the grower about the weedkillers used in the orchard the student discovers that yes, weedkillers were used very recently. However, the type of weedkiller used (discovered from asking the grower) is harmless to the young apple plants, a fact students should know.

Another observation that could lead to an alternative hypothesis involves nematodes (eelworms). Some species can damage the roots of plants. If soil is taken from the orchard and nematodes are extracted from this soil sample, many individuals are revealed! However, closer examination of the nematode mouthparts shows that these particular ones do not damage plants. The presence of non-damaging levels of pest mites and harmless fungi on the leaves completes the group of red herrings.

Step 6 – Add the non-essential components and so determine the boundary of the scenario

Storyboarding problem-based scenarios for students to work through creates a kind of virtual world. Potentially, students could be allowed to observe or do anything in this virtual world they would be able to do in the real world, even if it were not relevant to the problem at hand in any way. Including every person, object, place and task that might possibly exist in any given scenario environment is just not feasible. To do so would mean the scenario environment would take far too much time to create. However, at least some non-essential tasks and observations should be allowed, especially if they would be commonly undertaken when exploring some far-fetched hypotheses. These can be used to flesh out the scenario and add richness.

In our apple root rot scenario, students can examine spray equipment, talk to the neighbours and do many things that don't reveal anything, but nevertheless add to the richness of the experience. In another scenario, of course, these could indeed reveal something!

Step 7 – Add the content to each task and observation

Having determined exactly *which* tasks and observations students will be allowed to explore, the next step is to find the exact words and/or multimedia components that will be used. This is what the student will read, see or hear, and so what goes in here is very important. Some tips are:

a)   Collect the multimedia components

Whilst developing a scenario, bear in mind the availability of images, sound or video. These can add interest to the scenario. In some cases, they are highly important. For plant disease diagnosis, for example, a picture really does "paint a thousand words". Although the choice of photographs can emphasise (or de-emphasise) a certain diagnostic feature, they are better than textual descriptions for allowing the student to carry out the interpretation. Scan or collect appropriate images both for the clues and red herrings.

Video can be used to show a diagnostic feature. For example, leaf roller caterpillars are damaging pests to many crops. When disturbed the larvae wriggle violently. This is a diagnostic characteristic of the pest that can be captured with video. Video is also excellent for showing human body language, which may be important for scenarios where part of the assessment requires this to be interpreted.

Finally, video, sound and images simply add to the realism of the scenario. The more you can illustrate the problem, the better. Bear in mind, however, that multimedia component, especially video, is expensive to produce both in time and money. For video and audio, people with an acting bent might be required. It would pay therefore, to initially collect or produce multimedia components critical to the analysis, before adding extras just for richness.

b)   Decide on how much interpretation is inherent in the observation

Decide how much help you would like to give students when returning the results of an observation or test. For example, I have developed a schools version of the apple root rot scenario, and one that is used by third-year-university-level crop protection students. When the latter students send off leaves, they simply get back a series of nutrient values, e.g. 1.5% of dry matter. It is up to the students to decide whether this is significant or not. On the other hand, in the schools version, the returned lab analysis states, "The nitrogen looks a little low". In other words, the scenario author has already interpreted some of the facts for the student.

c)   Insert some humour

Humour should be an essential element of all scenarios. It simply adds enjoyment and makes the scenario fun to work through. For example, in the apple root rot scenario, the grower is played by an actor and presented in a series of video clips. He has a distinct personality and accent; he is a colourful character. Relayed textual observations can also be written in a humorous style, that conveys interesting word-pictures. For example, the introductory text for the root rot scenario concludes with "The grower remains beside you, his appearance stoic, despite his seemingly impending bankruptcy!"

Step 8 – Decide if any task or observation should encounter a cost, or a penalty

In the real world, things cost money. Any investigative process normally involves spending … on travel, phone calls, hours worked, research and tests. If problem-based scenarios are mirroring the real world, why should these costs be absent?

In many of our scenarios, we add a cost to expensive tasks such as lab procedures and give our students a budget. We find this is good for "focusing the mind" and getting students to really question whether doing that task, even though it is available and could possibly strengthen the hypothesis, is actually worth the money required.

For example, in the apple root rot scenario, students have the option of carrying out a nutrient analysis of the leaves. It's an expensive procedure, costing about $100. If they choose it, they discover that the leaf nutrients are low; hardly surprising, given their appearance. This adds weight to the hypothesis of a root problem, but no more than just looking at other factors (the ineffective drainage, the tree symptoms etc.) The (expensive) test is not a very definitive one; hence it is not really worth the money.

Step 9 – Compile the feedback and debrief

Much of the learning students achieve through my problem-based scenario exercises comes from the debriefing where their analysis and recommendations are critiqued and/or from feedback they are given as they attempt particular tasks. It is important for teachers to provide this in abundance, pointing out the salience of each significant observation, and explaining which alternative hypotheses could be formulated and why they could be rejected or at least thought less likely. This is where much of the learning takes place, as it gives the student the opportunity to reflect on any mistakes.

Step 10 – Test your scenarios

The last step is to give your scenario a test run with some willing evaluators. Graduate students, friends, consultants and other staff members are all good candidates. They will be able to give you feedback as to how easy or hard the exercise was, and point out any inconsistencies.

A summary of general principles

Scenario creation occurred by trial and error, but over the 12 years of my using this approach some general principles and strategies seem to work. In short, these are:

1. Define the learning objectives
2. Decide on a scenario
3. Determine how the scenario will be presented
4. Outline a sensible investigative pathway
5. Allow alternative hypotheses to be explored
6. Determine the boundary of the scenario
7. Add the content to each task and observation (using multimedia and humour), deciding how much assistance you will give the students with **interpretation**
8. Decide on costs or penalties for particular tasks or observations
9. Compile the feedback and debriefing
10. Test the scenarios.

Conclusion

Problem-based scenarios solved a teaching problem for me. Giving my students "essential slices of reality" allowed them to experience a field diagnosis of a crop condition, something many of them would be faced with once leaving university. In this virtual setting, they could interrogate, explore, make mistakes and learn.

In developing and using problem-based scenarios, I have become a strong believer in the usefulness of this approach in teaching generally.

References

Savery, J. R. and Duffy, T. M. (1995), 'Problem-based learning: An instructional model and its constructivist framework', *Educational Technology,* vol.35, no. 5, pp.31–38.

Stewart, T.M. (2002), 'Diagnosis for crop protection' [Online] Available *http://www.diagnosis.co.nz* (1 May 2002).

Stewart, T.M., Kemp, R. and Bartrum, P. (2001), 'Computerised problem-based scenarios in practice – A decade of DIAGNOSIS', *Proceedings of ICALT 2001: International Conference on Advanced Learning Technologies,* USA: IEEE Computer Society, pp. 153–156.

Stewart, T.M. (2002), 'CHALLENGE. A problem-based scenario authoring system' [Online] Available *http://challenge.massey.ac.nz* (1 May 2002).

Shank, R.C. (1996), 'Goal-based scenarios. Case-based reasoning meets learning by doing', in Leake, D.B. (ed.), *Case-based Reasoning: Experiences, Lessons and Future Directions,* USA: AAAI Press/The MIT Press.

8

Rather than being told: Using SBL to raise cultural awareness in nurse education

Moira McLoughlin, Christine Hogg and Angela Darvell

Introduction

In 1997 preparation began for the development of a new module to facilitate cultural awareness in nurse education. Problem-based learning as a component of scenario-based learning (SBL) was the chosen learning and teaching strategy for this module, entitled 'Cultural awareness in nursing' (see box below). The overarching personal philosophy of facilitators for the module was the desire to equip students to meet the cultural needs of patients and clients by enabling the students to develop awareness and skills to meet the nursing needs of a multicultural client group.

The Module: Cultural Awareness in Nursing

The module is situated in the final semester on the students' course and is the first experience of SBL for the students. The students are drawn from mental health, child and adult branches of pre-registration nurse education. Each group is then representative of all three branches for the purpose of the SBL. Alavi (1999) recommends group size should be no larger than fifteen members. The three lecturers alternate their position as facilitator and observer. Assessment is formative, including portfolio development linked to clinical practice, and presentations of evidence.

This chapter outlines some of the issues surrounding the development and implementation of this module and the use of scenarios to trigger learning about cultural issues.

Context

Significant learning occurs as a component of authentic activities that are common to the community of practice in which the learner is involved. Therefore, preparing student nurses to deliver health care in a multicultural society is an essential task in nurse education (OPCS, 1992; McGee, 1994; Gerrish, Husband and MacKenzie, 1996; Holland and Hogg, 2001). At the outset of this development there were four individuals interested in using SBL as a teaching and learning strategy. Reviewing the literature related to student-centred learning strategies indicated a need for paradigm shifts in teaching and learning (Rolfe, 1996, Glen and Wilkie, 2000, Savin-Baden, 2000). Researchers advocated new methods of teaching and learning, proposing that the teacher become facilitator and students become increasingly self-directed learners (Savin Baden, 1996; Wilkie, 1999). This use of student-centred approaches to learning was also reflected in national policy recommendations in the United Kingdom, (ENB, 1994, 1997; UKCC, 1994; NCIHE, 1997; DoH, 1999). There was an associated need for a paradigm shift in new curriculum development and for teaching materials to be revised and re-evaluated. Conway (2000) argues that curriculum development needs to occur through a paradigm that articulates and emphasises:

- selection of content from practice
- concepts as the organising structure of the curriculum
- process as content

Development

The development team for this module had achieved success with a teaching and learning quality improvement scheme (TLQIS) bid at the university. This included preparing core teaching and learning materials to enhance the quality of student learning for those undertaking the cultural awareness module. Modular aims and key competencies were written to reflect the importance of students' bringing real issues from practice for discussion in an attempt to raise their cultural awareness (see box below)

List of Key Competencies

The module development team felt it was essential that students develop key competencies in relation to meeting the cultural needs of clients. These key competencies were identified as the ability to:

- communicate effectively
- challenge stereotypes and assumptions
- understand and recognise personal and institutional racism
- understand people in the widest social and economic context
- disseminate knowledge and cultural aspects of care to peers and other healthcare professionals
- recognise and understand pertinent legislation
- recognise inequalities in service provision, which may limit access to quality healthcare.

Initially the team designed a trigger (see Rubena trigger) in partnership, the Rubena scenario, with practitioners who had a specific interest in cultural awareness. These practitioners were encouraged to bring real-life dilemmas that were examples of cultural issues regularly being encountered in clinical practice. The scenarios were necessarily ambiguous to provoke exploration of the issues and knowledge base of individual students. The focus of the initial meetings centred on the logistics of using this teaching and learning strategy and, to some extent our own developmental needs as facilitators. Preparing a lesson plan and lecture notes in isolation to deliver a particular topic to meet modular learning outcomes might seem easier than facilitating learning with the use of scenarios.

We needed to ascertain the students' current level of knowledge in order to match their needs. This scenario (trigger) assumed that the students had previously been exposed to young Asian women and to people who harm themselves/overdose as a means of communicating extreme distress. Students were encouraged to use their prior insight and knowledge. With the Rubena scenario students quickly recognised the problems and challenges in caring for young women presenting as apparent victims of self-harm and alerted us to media stories (always prevalent in the local press). In one case a student was keen to share with us her experiences of living in a mixed-race marriage and the issues of bringing up young people in a multicultural society.

Contemporary nursing practice demands skills in developing evidence-based knowledge to support clinical decision-making. Therefore student nurses must develop skills in their learning that can be transferred to caring for patients in a practice-based setting. If universities are espousing the idea of liberal education, that is, liberal in the sense of 'liberating', then it is vitally important to prepare students to learn how to learn and to learn how to think critically, on their own and in collaboration with others (Facione, 1997).

The main challenge was ensuring that this could be achieved, as the problems associated with teaching cultural awareness in nursing and healthcare are well documented (McGee, 1992; Papadopoulos, Alleyne and Tilki, 1994). Past methods have been criticised for relying on 'transmission-ist' styles, which are essentially reductionist in nature and often do not allow students to explore complex and challenging issues that arise (Freire, 1972; Schon, 1987). It can be argued that this approach may foster stereotypical perceptions of other cultures – these are often perceptions that are prescriptive in nature, viewing patients and families not as individuals with individual needs but as a problematic homogeneous group.

Compounding this issue is a national picture that suggests that the preparation of healthcare practitioners is ad hoc in its approach and largely inadequate (Gerrish *et al.*, 1996). Developing an awareness of the cultural needs of individuals is considered to be an essential prerequisite for working in today's National Health Service (NHS) due to the need to ensure equality in caregiving and offer equal opportunities for carers (Gerrish *et al.*, 1996; Beishon, Virdee and Hagell, 1995; Baxter, 1997; Holland and Hogg, 2001). The School of Nursing is committed to this equality through its philosophy and its practice.

Triggers

Wilkie (2000) uses the term "trigger" and suggests that it is the initial stimulus used to introduce each scenario. The issues of 'problem relevance' were underlined by the clinician who claimed that this case study was based on an amalgam of several clients on his caseload. By changing the name and other details we could assure confidentiality (UKCC, 1996; NMC, 2002).

Designing and writing scenarios for this module was a task that in many ways we were unprepared for, not being current practitioners. To some extent we were quite naïve in the assumption that triggers would present themselves or would be formulated quickly by this team. Drummond-Young and Mohide (2001:165) suggest that triggers should focus student learning, arouse students' interest in the content and provide meaningful context within which prior learning is activated and new knowledge gained. The scenario was written in such a way that it met the needs of students undertaking the three discreet branches of nursing; for example, the scenario involved the sort of patient or client that might be encountered in all settings, and reflected real-life practice. In retrospect we had failed to consider the complex and challenging issues around scenario design and the need to test out and refine them with clinical practitioners. David *et al.* (1999:29) suggest a structure for designing problems, maintaining that it should follow a particular sequence that includes a feedback loop to the module design team from facilitators. The trigger we are using to illustrate the complexities of design is as follows.

The Rubena Scenario Trigger

Rubena is a 15-year-old young woman who is admitted to the hospital ward after taking an overdose of 10 paracetamol tablets the previous night. On the ward she is quiet and withdrawn and visibly upset. In the Accident and Emergency Department, Rubena has said that she wants to die. This is reportedly following an argument with her father last night about her hair. Rubena lives at home with her parents and her two brothers. She attends the local school, where she is doing well.

David *et al.* (1999) suggest that a scenario should be striking and leave an impression on student memories. In this way students discover what they need to learn, which often incorporates elements of self-direction that foster a 'deep' as opposed to 'surface' approach to their learning (Marton, 1975; Marton and Säljö, 1976a; Marton and Säljö, 1976b). 'Rubena' was designed in co-operation with a clinical nurse specialist who was consulted with regards to typical case scenarios. The aim was to allow the students to explore the complexities of living and growing up in a multicultural society and to understand the needs of young women using self-harm as a method of coping with extreme distress.

We introduce the scenario with a statement such as "Today you are coming to work on an early shift and this is your patient in bed four." This was to encourage the students to form a mental picture of a patient they might encounter that very morning.

This structure loosely followed the learning objectives for the module, 'that students should be able to work co-operatively and across their different branches of nursing', i.e. child, adult and mental health. In the spirit of the curriculum this is akin to shared learning, a teaching and learning strategy – encouraging students to come together as "nurses first", with exploration of the commonalties of the three branches of nursing. The aim is to encourage greater co-operation and partnership in future clinical practice and to encourage greater understanding of how different healthcare professionals work. It was anticipated that this particular trigger would be relevant to all branches of nursing. Mental health nurses frequently come into contact with young women such as Rubena as self-harm is considered a mental health issue. But because of her age and diagnosis, Rubena may well be admitted to a children's hospital or children's ward in a general hospital to receive care for her physical health problems. In this situation children's nurses may complain about their lack of knowledge and skills in caring for young people who harm themselves, and may point out their lack of knowledge of mental health interventions.

Alternatively, young women such as Rubena could be admitted to an accident and emergency room as the first port of call in emergency care. This is potentially a difficult healthcare situation for many adult health nurses, who often argue that they feel ill-equipped to care for young people presenting with mental health needs. Often nurses in this situation are reported to avoid patients who harm themselves for fear of "saying the wrong thing" and thus "making things worse" (Babiker and Arnold, 1997).

The issue – self-harm in young Asian women – is of particular importance in the UK and is of growing concern. It has been highlighted in national documents (DoH, 2000; Balarajan and Raleigh, 1992). They indicate that the suicide rate in women in the 20–49 years age group born in the Indian subcontinent is 21 per cent higher than that of the general population. Evidence demonstrates that people often encounter negative and stigmatising attitudes and, as a consequence, punitive treatments (Babiker and Arnold, 1997). People who self-harm are often labelled as "attention seeking" or "manipulative".

Evaluation

Students were invited to provide feedback on module evaluation forms and to be part of focus groups. The module evaluations were overwhelmingly positive and when examined in depth revealed encouraging results. Focus group transcripts were transcribed and analysed using thematic content analysis (Coliazzi, 1978). Findings were extremely positive, with four clear categories emerging:

- ownership of learning
- praxis of nursing
- self-development
- knowledge acquisition.

The students reported that knowledge acquisition seemed to be deeper and richer in comparison to their prior experiences with the traditional face-to-face teaching method.

Many reported a motivation to continue their acquisition of knowledge and requested further input after registering as nurses.

What then are some of the implications for those of us working with teachers who want to, or will, become facilitators using scenarios to trigger learning?

There appear to be three basic issues

1. The role of the facilitator is crucial to success. It is essential to stress facilitation skills, because the effectiveness of the teacher as facilitator is a critical component of/in the success of this learning and teaching style.
2. It is important to consider the relationships among teachers' beliefs about teaching and learning, classroom practices, and changes in student learning.
3. It may be difficult for teachers to make the significant changes in teaching and learning; therefore, they themselves must be supported as learners.

McLoughlin (2002), in a study of the transition from lecturer to facilitator in a PBL curriculum, found that the difficulties often lie in 'letting go'. The 'sage on the stage' finds it difficult to move to 'guide on the side' (Woods, 1994). As a developmental team we have found that using this teaching and learning strategy has proven to be an extremely valuable learning process in terms of not just what students gain from the process, but what we as facilitators discovered about our facilitation styles.

Reflexivity

Overall, the most important factor in the design of the trigger was to keep the scenario relatively short but allow sufficient time to encourage depth and the stimulation of active learning and enquiry. Indeed this scenario/trigger allows for sufficient brainstorming and hypothesis generation. The issues around hair-cutting, for example, encourage students to think about possible reasons for an argument ensuing between Rubena and her father. Is this linked in some way to adolescent development? Some students are quick to jump to the conclusion that Rubena has cut off her hair, and this is related to the stereotype that all Asian women have long hair. Other students point out that Rubena may have dyed her hair and that this has caused an argument.

These dialogues were extremely important, and facilitators should be aware of using these situations as prompts to learning taking place. When students were formulating the learning issues from the scenario they were encouraged to examine the cultural and social symbolism of hair in both Western and Eastern cultures and societies. Others explored the issue of hair from a feminist perspective.

Also important in scenario design was that some issues were deliberately left open to allow the students to discover the limits of their knowledge, for example about names and naming systems. In the first instance some of the students protested that they should be allowed information about the origin of the name before they could proceed to researching and seeking information. They believed "they should be told". Together we noted that in clinical situations information is often not readily available, and in reality, healthcare professionals sometimes have to use clinical reasoning skills in the absence of vital information. We advised that they should use clues that are not explicit, such as dress. They conceded that it would also be prudent to investigate the origin of the name prior to launching into their studies. Interestingly the name was judged to be a typical Muslim name by one group, and a typical Jewish name by another group. In both cases, the assumptions made about Rubena met the learning needs of this scenario and fitted their concerns about issues in practice. The name originally was chosen to reflect a south Asian derivation but we decided to let the students run with their other choices.

The following is a list of learning needs identified by the students over the course of this module:

- Family life in South Asian communities. What are the roles and gender issues?
- What's in a name? Naming systems and culture
- How to care for people who have overdosed/self -harm
- Communication skills with young people
- Suicide/para-suicide: what is the difference?
- Young people and self-harm: reason and rationales
- The liver size and functions, normal pathology, overdose and toxic overdose
- Gender and mental health
- Assessment and risk assessment
- Hair – cultural and symbolic representations
- Suicide and religion
- Islam and women
- Judaism and women
- Child and adolescent mental health issues.

The students are also encouraged to set themselves a learning objective for individual learning contracts in practice, such as:

> Discuss the issues (from the Rubena trigger) in relation to family life in South Asian communities and the impact of self-image and identity on adolescents.

Students in this module are encouraged to actively research their topic, not only by using databases and current research evidence but also by going out to visit practitioners or by interviewing people in the community. In one particular instance a student asked permission and interviewed an Asian couple about living in the United Kingdom in the twentieth and twenty-first century. They owned the local shop and she had known them for several years, but her presentation to the group revealed issues related to their healthcare encounters in the UK that she had never spoken to them about before.

During feedback we also used questions to act as prompts such as:

- Suppose Rubena was Yusuf?
- Does Rubena want to die?
- What is the first thing you would say and do to Rubena and why?
- How does Rubena's mother feel?

What did the students say?

"Now, I think I understand how difficult it must be for people like this, in this position. It's like having two worlds ... living in two worlds."

"I'm going to work where people are admitted with liver damage from drinking and overdosing and, this has been so interesting."

"It's funny to see things from other people's viewpoint – you know like the mental health nurses see overdoses differently to us (adult nurses)."

"Yeah it's taught me a lot ... about tolerance and things ...."

"It's weird; I never gave hair a second thought before today."

Students were actively encouraged to draw upon their own experiences, explore them in the small group, reflect upon them and subsequently develop practice as a result of this discourse. This is underpinned in work by Schon (1987), who stressed the need to place practice at the centre of knowledge and to learn by focusing on real-life situations which are grounded in reality.

Conclusion

Scenario-based learning was adopted as an educational approach to student learning that involved teachers and practitioners developing a module to reflect real-life practice situations. A great advantage of choosing it was that students were able to independently explore issues in relation to cultural awareness at a deeper level, and able to draw upon knowledge and ideas that they owned as individuals. However, this knowledge is generated within the mind of the individual and cannot be transferred from one person to another.

The module has now been running twice a year since July 1999; six cohorts of students have chosen to do it with 20 students in each cohort.

We feel that the overall ethos of the module has allowed students to explore and discuss "live" matters and dilemmas in relation to cultural issues that they encounter in practice. This has been a steep learning curve for the facilitators, who have been involved from the outset, but one that has enriched their teaching and facilitation styles both personally and professionally.

References

Alavi, C. (1995), *Problem-based learning in a health sciences curriculum*, London: Routledge Press.

Babiker, G. and Arnold, L. (1997), *The language of injury. Comprehending self-mutilation*, Reading: British Psychological Society.

Balarajan, V. and Raleigh, R. (1992), 'Suicide levels and trends among immigrants in England and Wales', *Health Trends*, vol. 24, pp. 91–94.

Barrows, H. (1986), 'A taxonomy of problem-based learning methods', *Medical Education*, vol. 20, pp. 481–486.

Baxter, C. (1997), *Race equality in health care and education*, London: Bailliere Tindall/ Royal College of Nursing.

Beishon, S. Virdee, S. and Hagell, A. (1995), *Nursing in a multi-ethnic NHS*, London: Policy Studies Institute.

Conway, J. (2000), 'From practice to theory: Reconceptualising curriculum development for PBL', in Seng, T.O., Little, P., Yin, H.S. and Conway, J. (eds), *Problem-based learning: Educational innovation across disciplines: A collection of selected papers*, Temasek, Singapore: Temasek Centre for Problem-based Learning.

David, T., Patel, L., Burdett, K. and Rangachari, P. (1999), *Problem-based learning in medicine. A practical guide for students and teachers*, London: The Royal Society of Medicine Press.

Department of Health (1999), *Making a difference: Strengthening the nursing, midwifery and health visiting contribution to health and health care*, London: HMSO.

Department of Health (2000), *National service framework for mental health*, London: HMSO.

Drummond-Young, M. and Mohide, E.A. (2001), 'Developing problems for use in Problem-based learning', in Rideout, E. (ed.), *Transforming nursing education through problem-based learning*, London: Jones and Bartlett Publishers.

Miller, C., Jones, M. and Tomlinson, A. (1994), 'The current teaching provision for individual learning styles of students on pre-registration diploma programmes in adult nursing', *Research Highlights*, November 1994, London: ENB.

English National Board for Nursing Midwifery and Health Visiting (1997), *Standards for approval of higher education institutions and programmes*, London: English National Board.

Facione, P. (1997), *Critical thinking: What it is and why it counts*, California: California Academic Press.

Freire, P. (1972), *Pedagogy of the oppressed*, Harmondsworth: Penguin.

Gerrish, K. Husband, C. and Mackenzie, J. (1996), 'An examination of the extent to which pre-registration programmes of nursing and midwifery education prepare practitioners to meet the healthcare needs of minority ethnic communities', *Research Highlights*. June 1996, London: English National Board.

Glen, S. and Wilkie, K. (ed.) (2000), *PBL in nursing: A new model for a new context*, London: Macmillan Press.

Holland, K. and Hogg, C. (2001), *Cultural awareness in nursing and health care – An introductory text*, Arnold: London.

Marton, F. (1975), 'What does it take to learn?', in Entwistle, N. and Hounsell, D. (eds), *How students learn*, Lancaster: Institute for Research and Development in Post Compulsory Education.

Marton, F. and Saljo, R. (1976a), 'On qualitative differences in learning. I Outcome and process', *British Journal of Educational Psychology*, vol. 46, pp.4–11.

Marton, F. and Säljö, R. (1976b), 'On qualitative differences in learning: II. Outcome as a function of the learner's conception of the task', *British Journal of Educational Psychology*, vol. 46, pp.115–27.

McGee, P. (1992), *Teaching transcultural care: A guide for teachers of nursing and healthcare*, London: Chapman and Hall.

McGee, P. (1994), 'Educational issues in transcultural nursing', *British Journal of Nursing*, vol.3, pp.1113–1116.

McLoughlin, M. (2002), 'An exploration of the role of the problem-based learning facilitator: Paradigm shift or new ways of working'. Unpublished MSc dissertation. Huddersfield: Huddersfield University.

National Committee of Inquiry into Higher Education (1997), 'Higher Education in the learning society', *Report of the National Committee*. Norwich, UK: HMSO.

Nursing and Midwifery Council (2002), *Code of Professional Conduct*. London: NMC.

Office of Population Censuses and Surveys (1992), *Census for Great Britain*, London: HMSO.

Papadopoulos, I., Alleyne, J. and Tilki, M. (1994), 'Promoting transcultural care in a College of healthcare studies', *British Journal of Nursing*. Vol. 3, no. 21, pp.116–118.

Rolfe, G. (1996), *Closing the theory–practice gap: A new paradigm for Nursing*, Oxford: Butterworth-Heinemann.

Savin-Baden, M. (1996), 'Problem-based learning: a catalyst for enabling and disabling disjunction – prompting transitions in learner stances?' Unpublished PhD thesis, University of London Institute of Education.

Savin-Baden, M. (2000), *Problem-based learning in higher education: Untold stories*, Buckingham: Open University Press.

Schon, D.A. (1987), *The reflective practitioner. How professionals think in action*, New York: Basic Books.

UKCC (1994), *The future of professional practice*, London: United Kingdom Central Council.

UKCC (1996), *Guidelines for professional practice*, London: United Kingdom Central Council.

UKCC (2001), *Fitness for practice and purpose*, London: United Kingdom Central Council.

Wilkie, K. (1999), 'Facilitation skills in problem-based learning', Paper presented at the Qualitative Evidence-Based Practice Conference, Coventry University, UK, 15–17 May.

Wilkie, K. (2000), 'The nature of PBL', in Glen, S. and Wilkie, K. (eds), *PBL in Nursing: A new model for a new context*, London: Macmillan Press.

Woods, D. R. (1994), *Problem-based learning: How to gain the most from PBL*, McMaster University: McMaster University Bookstore.

9

Craving (un)certainty: Using SBL for teaching diversity in health care contexts

Eula Miller, Sophie Smailes, Sheila Stark, Clare Street and Katherine Watson

Introduction

We have recently introduced scenario-based learning (SBL) as a learning and teaching strategy on a module entitled 'Health care for a diverse population' that forms part of two programmes within a Health Care Studies department. The programmes are the DipHE, pre-registration nursing and the BA (Hons) Health and Social Care (BAHSC). Our philosophy with respect to teaching diversity centres on enabling students to develop layered 'readings' of often contextual situations within which diversity resides; in other words, we want them to be able to look beyond the surface descriptors (first layer) and start to 'unpack' and critically analyse the complexities and context of real lives. Alternative teaching approaches to the prescriptive anti-discriminatory sessions were explored, but it was felt that SBL had the potential to destabilise the idea of 'fixed' (or 'right') answers. This approach offers students a contextual framework to examine and critically reflect upon issues of diversity in relation to themselves, their roles as health care professionals and health care practice as a whole.

We encountered a number of pedagogical issues when utilising SBL. These primarily reflected the students' resistance to alternative and uncertain methods of learning and teaching. This chapter outlines some of the issues that we have faced in the development and implementation of SBL.

Context

Diversity has contemporary, personal, academic and professional resonance for us, as a multi-disciplinary research and teaching team. We believe that concepts such as racism, homophobia, sexism and marginalisation are difficult to really understand and learn since they are situated in a turbulent, chaotic and messy everyday context. Further, they are hinged around fluid concepts of identity. The essentialist allocation of membership to any given group such as gay, Asian or disabled fails to meet an individual's needs, as it can lead to the privileging of one 'identity' over others; for example, disability may be privileged over gender, class and sexuality. In reality, individuals take their identity from many sources (Karlsen and Nazroo, 2000; Yoder, 2000). Any brand of essentialism, therefore, is not subtle enough to capture multi-layered and complex identities, as essentialism tends to rely on homogenising or 'privileging' identity.

Thus, when developing the module, we were very aware of the temptation to fall into prescriptive sessions – 'How to do' health and social care with … 'disabled people, black communities, lesbians and gay men', etc. Looking at textbook examples of anti-discriminatory practice in social work for example (Thompson, 1997; Appleby and Anastas, 1998), reveals the tendency to resort to formulaic solutions, which are bound by self-monitored politically correct ideologies and rhetoric. We believe these, in turn, can be used as a substitute for critical analysis and engagement.

SBL has the potential of capturing the complex, multi-layered nature of situations where the implicit notion of the existence of neat, uncomplicated, and uncontroversial responses and solutions to problems can be challenged (Savin-Baden, 2000). Students can start to recognise that 'solutions' vary according to context, "… learning and life take place in contexts, contexts which affect the kind of solutions that are available and possible" (Savin-Baden, 2000: 5). The scenarios, therefore, were designed to reflect these considerations and facilitate space in which students could question the 'story' itself and their responses. For us, it was the *process* that provided the learning experience, rather than the outcome.

Development

We collaboratively wrote the scenarios to reflect our, and our students', professional and personal knowledge and experiences. All the scenarios were taken from real-life events, although the development process differed (see Boxes 1 & 2). Students on the pre-registration nursing programme were invited to share actual experiences, of particular significance to them, of working with/caring for individuals with diverse health care needs. These experiences were used to jointly construct a scenario that enabled students to further explore issues that they felt were central to their personal and professional development around dealing with diversity. The decision to instigate an issue was thus student-led. For the BAHSC students (who are not on a professional training programme), the scenarios were either a composite of multi-disciplinary fieldwork or taken directly from research. All scenarios provided an opportunity to explore the multi-layered 'reading' of real life.

Aims

The aims, for both courses, were to encourage students to:

- explore issues of diversity, e.g. norms and values, stereotypes, discrimination (overt, covert) and the discourses that underpin health and social care practice
- reflect on the everyday 'messiness' of living in a socially and culturally diverse society
- consider how their, and others', experiences of reality influence decision-making processes

- build and develop existing knowledge, skills and attitudes when caring for individuals from diverse cultural backgrounds
- develop insight into how differing health professionals' decisions and approaches may impact on the quality of patient care.

Box 1: Group One

Student group
- Pre-registration Nursing Student Adult branch. Level of study for module – novice.
- Age range 19–30
- Number of student participants: six
- All female: 20% African-Caribbean, 80% variety of white ethnic/cultural backgrounds.

Practice Issue / Scenario

A Muslim man, aged 43, was admitted to hospital after collapsing whilst out shopping with his family. A diagnosis of myocardial infarction was made. Within two days of being admitted he was labelled an 'uncooperative' patient, because he would not accept medication as prescribed, wanted his meals at unusual times and had 'hoards' of visitors.

Set-up
Initially the experience had been reported back to a group of 14 students; six participants opted to look into this issue as it was of particular interest to them.

In order for the diverse health needs of this individual to be met appropriately the six participants and the facilitator discussed and decided who they felt key people involved in care should be.

Two students were asked to find out information, utilising any source, with respect to cultural beliefs in relation to health care.

Two students were allocated the task of investigating the role of nurses and health care assistants in potentially enhancing the care given.

Two students were allocated the task of investigating the role of medical staff in care, and how pre-discharge planning and information could enhance care for the patient within the community setting.

Box 2: Group Two

Student group
- Level one undergraduate students on a generic degree programme in health and social care.
- 90% are 18/19 years old, 10% are mid 20s to late 30s
- prior learning and experience largely located in a variety of further education courses
- 92% female, 8% male
- 35% south Asian, 8% African Caribbean and Chinese, 57% variety of white ethnic/cultural backgrounds.

Development of the scenarios
- jointly written by the tutors
- a composite of multidisciplinary fieldwork and published research
- issues of diversity were foregrounded.

Scenarios

Scenario one – Maria Briggs is a 28-year-old woman, who lives in privately rented accommodation in North Manchester. She is a single mother of three children (aged, 3, 5 and 7) and on benefits. Her children are on the child protection register and the authorities are exploring options regarding the appropriate response to the situation.

Scenario two – Nita and Clare are a lesbian couple in their 30s who have been together for 8 years. Nita is a British Asian woman of Indian descent & Clare is white British with English/Irish heritage. They see themselves as middle class; both work part-time, Clare as a teacher and Nita in an Asian women's community project. They have successfully adopted three Asian girls, and have applied to another authority to be fosterers for seven Asian sisters. (Adapted from Hicks, 2000.)

Set up

Students were asked to
- sort themselves into small groups (approx 7)
- read through the scenarios individually
- work together over a specified period of time to consider the issues raised.

Scenario one asked students to consider four 'professional' reports detailing responses to Maria's circumstances.

Scenario two asked students to take on the guise of an official decision-making panel. Both scenarios required them to concentrate on process and outcome.

Evaluation

Students were invited to provide feedback on completion of the exercise. The pre-registration nursing students set up an informal 45-minute focus group, during which they discussed the learning process, working relationships, perspectives and needs. A similar exercise was done in class with the BAHSC students, who were asked to discuss the issues raised amongst themselves, without tutor facilitation, and give feedback in the form of an anonymous written summary. The evaluations have highlighted a number of issues in terms of both the philosophies underpinning our teaching (and use of SBL) and some areas of resistance from our students. These are outlined below.

Active, experiential vs. traditional, didactic methods of teaching and learning

We have been committed throughout this project to exploring some of the ways that we can destabilise the students' search for concrete answers and reliance on tutor 'expertise'. We questioned the effectiveness of traditional teaching and learning methods in facilitating students' engagement with the themes of diversity.

Using SBL has been one way to subvert this relationship of dependency and highlight the unreliable nature of 'knowledge' when dealing with a diverse population. It encourages students to explore the *variety* of possible outcomes to any given scenario (based on their own and other dominant ideas about the 'people on the page') and examine the range of possible discourses and competing stories, rather than expecting concrete 'how to do … ' answers.

Our experience of using the scenarios proved both positive and negative in this respect. On the surface the students did engage with this more fluid, and student-centred, approach to learning. Students on the pre-registration nursing programme had a high level of involvement and self-direction almost immediately because they had provided the direction of the scenario in the first instance. As a group they were able to structure information sharing and gathering, setting tasks for further research. They clearly drew on their personal 'knowledge', and experience within professional practice, to challenge and question the status quo as presented in the scenarios, suggesting creative and inclusive strategies.

The health and social care students who were asked to consider composite scenarios were also able to engage with this process. Although they relied more heavily on prior learning of theoretical concepts and knowledge to 'deconstruct' the stories, they worked collaboratively and came up with reasoned assessments of each scenario.

However, there were some sources of tension relating to this method of teaching that have to do with expected modes of teaching and learning. The pre-registration nurses 'craved' tutor input and felt uncomfortable with the shift in the tutor/student roles, feeling that it was "a long-winded way of learning" – something that the tutor could have told them in one (didactic) session. Even though the tutor emphasised in the preamble to the work that there were no 'rights and wrongs', many of the students were not sure that they came up with the 'correct' answer(s). There was still an expectation that we, the tutors, would provide *the* answer.

The importance of facts

For some groups the absence of 'facts' created difficulties.

It was hard making decisions based on such a small amount of information.

The decision was not made, due to lack of knowledge and information about the case.

Fact-finding was interesting, but wanted more direction as to where best sources of information could be acquired from.

They felt that they did not *know* enough or have enough *facts* at their fingertips, for instance, "we didn't know enough about Hinduism". In most cases, the students presented back to the group neatly packaged and 'sanitised' answers by leaving out the factual 'loose ends'. In the Nita and Claire scenario, all the students engaged in a weighing up process to come to their decisions. One group, for example, decided that, despite the lesbian relationship, a proper home for the children where they could all be together was more beneficial than any harm that might come from the relationship. Being financially stable, middle-class professionals was seen as a counterbalance to what they still saw as the deviant sexuality of the couple (one group commented that "sexuality is only a small part of the process").

What is interesting about this, in the context of exploring a diverse population, is that we do not feel any decisions can be made on 'facts' alone. Facts do not exist in a 'values vacuum' (Seedhouse, 1997). Values and discourses shape how 'facts' are interpreted or selected. What the students failed to do, by and large, whilst working with these scenarios, was to critique the actual content, language and social constructs underpinning the possible (and dominant) 'readings' of the stories. Thus, issues such as sexuality, race and gender were still seen as problematic identities – albeit that these identities might be/were more favourably viewed in terms of equal opportunity (as in the example above).

Classroom culture and group dynamics

The group dynamics in the classroom was also an interesting feature of our experience of using SBL, where we were able to observe students interacting. With the BAHSC group, most of the students found it very difficult to organise themselves (physically) into group situations that might facilitate discussion. The students tended to set themselves up to face each other in a line, thus encouraging the potential for cliques and twosomes and creating difficulty in physically sharing ideas among the whole group.

This inability to organise themselves reflects again students' resistance to alternative ways of working in the classroom, but may also point to other issues around the diversity of the classroom group itself. Whilst the students seemed unaware of the fact that the issues, they were discussing have resonance both in and outside the classroom, they also monitored their responses and felt policed by the nature of the topic and by us as tutors. Students mostly treated the scenarios as relating purely to 'out there', rather than reflecting on their own experiences and group dynamics to inform the decision-making process.

This again was reiterated in their desire to find the 'right' answers. Students wondered about the degree to which their experiences in dealing with the scenario(s) had led them to adopt 'particular' opinions. They also questioned the extent to which the tutor's selection of study context had influenced their decision-making. This also possibly reflects the students' perceptions of the tutor's own political stances, as well as the perceived expectations of the module.

Students may be aware of (if not compliant with) what they perceive to be 'politically correct' ideas within their educational institution or professional body. This can be demonstrated by the very presence of modules such as Health Care for a Diverse Population and of government and community strategies and policies which address concepts such as equal opportunities (DoH, 1999; DoH, 2000; NHS Executive, 2000; UKCC, 2001). Given that students in higher education study in a climate which judges their performance by the conferment of criteria-led grades, venturing 'unacceptable opinions' or proposing divergent ideas may, therefore, feel perilous. Pierre Bourdieu's (1998) analysis of the relationship between practical reason (the ability of people to make sense of the situations they are confronted with in the social world) and the forms of reason promoted by the academy (the capacity to make rational judgements and, thus, 'solve' problems), seems pertinent here.

Political correctness may, therefore, seem to students to be a safe option as it not only seemingly provides simple formulaic solutions, but ones that are bounded by 'acceptable' political ideologies and argument. In any event, we found that students sanitised their responses, both within their group discussions and in their final presentations, in concurrence with current (politically correct and formulaic) ideas about diverse populations.

Role of the facilitator

Closely linked to the above theme were issues around the role of the facilitator. As mentioned previously, we, as tutors, felt that the students were monitoring their answers according to what they thought we wanted to hear. We felt that perhaps our own identities (as black, lesbian or women) were being used by the students as regulatory gauges. This necessarily has an effect on how we respond to the student process and how we position ourselves in the classroom.

Another aspect of this theme was the discernible gap between our *expectations* as tutors and the outcomes from the SBL sessions. Because we introduced the SBL late in the modules, we had expected the students to be able to recognise the fluidity of the process and to engage in what we thought was the most productive way of learning. For example, the research underpinning the Nita and Clare scenario (Hicks, 2000) suggested to us that the students should be questioning the assumption that Hinduism is anti-lesbian. Hicks and McDermott had already stated that there is:

> [A] danger of the white social work establishment adopting rigid and stereotypical definitions of communities, cultures and religions that are actually diverse and continually changing … Communities are much more diverse than their community or religious leaders suggest and social workers should not use narrow and racist definitions of what is acceptable in order to discriminate against black lesbian and gay carers. (Hicks and McDermott, 1999:154)

Using this as our conceptual framework possibly obscured our views of the students' own process in making sense of the scenarios.

Key learning points

We have found that using SBL has proven to be a valuable learning process in terms of not just what students gain from the process, but what we as tutors discovered about the *process* of unpacking diversity in the current educational climate. The direct educational benefits for the students can be summarised as that they:

- took on different roles and critically reflected on their professional roles
- co-operated well in the sharing of knowledge and the presentation of discussion
- were reflective in terms of prior module input, experience and research
- developed an understanding of the impact of decision-making and issues relating to group consensus
- began to challenge the status quo and question current practice.

However, we also found that SBL (usefully) highlighted a number of issues that we might not have picked up on if we had used more didactic teaching methods. For example, the students

- focused on facts, information and absolutes as necessary to decision-making
- wanted to provide a polished answer in the face of complex uncertainty
- required text-book 'how to do' advice from tutors (the pre-registration nurses for example wanted 'best practice' guidelines on diversity)
- foregrounded outcome over process, weighing up pros and cons of the scenario instead of questioning Health and Social Care discourses and exploring their own issues, experiences and biases.

As tutors, we may have contributed to the above by

- setting the students up as 'quasi-experts' by asking them to take on the role of the decision-making panel/ 'professional body'
- introducing SBL late in the module instead of building it in cumulatively to the whole process of learning
- having certain expectations about the 'outcome' of the scenarios.

Advice to colleagues using SBL

There are a number of issues we have reflected on as a group that will inform our future use of SBL and that may be useful to colleagues considering using SBL as a mode of facilitating learning within their place of work/institution.

Role of the tutor

Flexibility

As the role of the tutor within this mode of teaching is akin to that of facilitator, we felt there was a great need to be self-aware, creative, open and flexible in our outlook towards student responses. A lot of emphasis is placed on our ability to listen, observe, reflect and sensitively challenge our students 'findings' and accept a variety of approaches and outcomes. It would be so easy for us to impose our values inadvertently on the students' investigations, artificially curtailing their own discursive constructions, fact-finding and reflection. Students need 'space' to be individualistic, creative and autonomous in their learning. Understanding that our students are novice learners (albeit with the capacity to critically assess what they do know) goes some way to bridging the gap between our expectations and the capacities of our students.

Crediting process, not outcome

Students must be given sufficient flexibility and responsibility to find their own solutions and we as tutors must find ways of crediting this dialogical process (even if it doesn't 'fit' with our own ideas).

Managing conflict

Given the potential for conflict, tutors must feel confident in their ability to work with this instability. Conflict can be central to the learning process, so must be permitted. However, we as tutors also have a responsibility to prevent harm, so group interaction must be monitored within the context of an agreed set of ground rules that protect each individual's safety.

Practical issues

Valuing uncertainty

We all felt that our students needed *clear guidance* in the first instance about their roles and the purpose of SBL, but in retrospect we felt that we could have made clearer our desire for uncertainty, rather than the presentation of 'certain' outcomes ('polished' answers)! We have discussed, for example, the possibility of encouraging students to view the SBL as a puzzle or mystery where they, as the detectives, needed to seek out the possible variety of 'stories' that could be told and the range of possible outcomes based on these discourses.

Physical environment

In the classroom we also encourage students to rearrange their *physical environment* in order to facilitate interpersonal communication and co-operation, as individuals can easily be excluded from participation unless the dynamics of the classroom are addressed (having moveable chairs, for example, is essential to this process). The physical environment should include working away from the classroom base, with facilitated group work giving students the opportunity to engage in dynamic debate.

Research-based scenarios

One thing that we found worked well when writing the scenarios was using *research from the field* as a framework. The 'Nita and Claire' scenario, for example, was adapted directly from a PhD research project (Hicks 2000) with the author's consent. Use of 'real-world work' means that students have access to the theoretical explanations given by the author, as well as the methodological issues underpinning the research, giving them the opportunity to build their knowledge base and integrate a number of perspectives.

Conclusion

The process of working with SBL has elicited a number of responses for us as tutors which can be taken forward to develop this teaching/learning approach. We found that SBL is a model of learning and teaching that needs to be built into the course curricula and developed over time to enable students, and tutors, to engage more fully with this dynamic process. The humanistic philosophy encapsulated within this engagement is ideally suited to exploring issues of diversity and equipping the students with skills for lifelong learning – skills applicable to professional and personal development. As part of this learning process we would need to continue to challenge concepts of traditional didactic teaching methods and shift our role from 'tutor' to 'facilitator', while acknowledging, at the same time, the impact of prior learning methodologies on the students. We found that SBL is ideally placed to work with all these issues and to explore diversity within the context of the uncertainties of everyday real life.

References

Appleby, G. A. and Anastas, J. W. (1998), *Not just a passing phase: Social work with gay, lesbian and bisexual people,* New York: Columbia University Press.

Bourdieu, P. (1998), *Practical reason: On the theory of action,* Cambridge: Polity Press.

Department of Health (1999), *Making a difference,* London: The Stationery Office.

Department of Health (2000), *The race and equality agenda for the Department of Health,* London: The Stationery Office.

Hicks, S. (2000), 'New ethnicities, old prejudices: The construction of racial norms in the assessment of lesbian foster carers', Paper presented at Lancaster University, Under the Rainbow: Researching Lesbian and Gay Lives Conference, September 2001.

Hicks, S. and McDermott, J. (eds) (1999), *Lesbian and gay fostering and adoption: Extraordinary yet ordinary,* London: Jessica Kingsley Publishers.

Karlsen, S. and Nazroo, J.Y. (2000), 'Identity and structure: Rethinking ethnic inequalities in health', in Graham, H. (ed.), *Understanding health inequalities,* Milton Keynes: Open University Press.

NHS Executive (2000), *The vital connection: An equalities framework for the NHS,* London: The Stationery Office.

Savin-Baden, M. (2000), *Problem-based learning in higher education: Untold stories,* Milton Keynes: Open University Press.

Seedhouse, D. (1997), *Health promotion, philosophy, prejudice and practice,* Chichester: John Wiley & Sons.

Thompson, N. (1997), *Anti-discriminatory practice* (2nd ed.), Houndmills: Macmillan.

UKCC (2001), *Fitness for Practice and Purpose,* London: UKCC.

Yoder, E. (2000), 'The bridging approach: Effective strategies for teaching ethnically diverse nursing students', *Journal of Trans-cultural Nursing,* vol.12, no.4, pp.319–325.

Part Three

Issues-based Scenarios

10

Can we all just get along? Exploring cultural sensitivity through student-centred scenarios

Judith Bernanke

Introduction

Over the past several years I have been fine-tuning a scenario-based learning (SBL) activity that I use as an assessment for an intercultural communication paper. This paper, required as part of the Bachelor of Business Information degree, introduces business students to basic theories and issues in intercultural communication. The goals of the assessment that I have developed for this class is for students to show, in a scenario they create, how ethnocentrism can affect communication and to demonstrate more appropriate and culturally sensitive approaches to intercultural interaction. Originally, the scenario served merely as a vehicle for students to demonstrate their understanding of important cultural issues. Now, however, this scenario-based assessment has taken on a life of its own and has become an exciting class event.

Although SBL activities are regularly used in intercultural training programmes to practise interactive behaviours, what is different about this assignment is the creative freedom students are given to use their own experiences and knowledge as the basis for exploring complex concepts. While this process has been successful overall, there are some basic issues to consider when using SBL activities, especially when they are student-generated and serve as assessments. This chapter discusses the risks and benefits of SBL and considers an alternative way of addressing problems that are a typical part of a team-based assessment.

SBL in traditional intercultural training

One of the most significant influences on the way we interact and communicate with others, especially strangers, is our attitude towards them. According to Gudykunst and Kim, "*Everyone is ethnocentric to some degree*" (Italics in original) (1997:120). Ethnocentrism, the view that one's cultural group is superior to another cultural group, implies that one's own culture provides the standard for what is reasonable and correct in life and serves as the basis for judging other groups. Developing intercultural sensitivity and improving intercultural communication skills require reducing ethnocentrism, which sometimes necessitates a fundamental shift in deeply ingrained values and ideas. Learning to identify and analyse ethnocentric attitudes and being able to implement more appropriate behaviours are important skills for intercultural communicators. Having the opportunity to practise these skills in a supportive and less threatening environment is ideal. As a result, SBL activities play an important part in intercultural training to help participants develop desired skills.

One approach uses scenarios, or "critical incidents" (Brislin, Cushner, Cherrie and Yong, 1986), that describe the unsuccessful interaction of individuals from different cultures. Usually, the basis of these individuals' problem lies with some cultural misunderstanding or unintended misinterpretation of events. A number of alternative explanations follow the case study and readers select the one that best accounts for the problem from the point of view of the characters in the case study. The various choices are then discussed and compared with specific cultural information and concepts. This approach encourages participants to develop a more sophisticated understanding of different cultural values and perceptions and to include situational information, such as culturally specific issues, when interpreting or making attributions about people's behaviours (Cushner and Brislin, 1996; Gudykunst and Kim, 1997). Prepared case studies provide an excellent basis for discussion, and speculating on the cultural issues that may underlie behaviours and attitudes helps participants become more aware of alternative points of view and experiences.

Another type of SBL used in intercultural training is role-playing. Role-plays and simulations are useful for exploring the emotional experience of intercultural encounters and for practising alternative, more effective behaviours in a relatively non-threatening context. Usually trainees are provided with the scenarios for this process. For example, Brislin and Yoshida (1994) suggest a "scripted role-playing" approach using some of their critical incidents as intercultural situations for trainees to act out. Trainees volunteer to play the parts and decide what to say and what actions will take place. In another approach, Mullavey-O'Byrne (1994) provides case studies that consist of a brief description of the setting, along with individual role cards that describe the character and behaviours each participant will perform. These role cards are kept hidden from the other players in the drama. With both approaches, trainees receive some specific information and guidelines regarding the situation they are to enact. Then after a brief preparation time of between five and thirty minutes, participants are free to play their assigned parts as they wish. Usually, role-plays are followed by a debriefing, which consists of personal reflection about the activity or group discussions or a combination of these.

Risks to consider

Although role-playing activities are generally accepted as beneficial for intercultural education, there can be risks when using them. With this in mind some measures are recommended to protect the well-being of participants and make the experience worthwhile:

Establish trust and a sense of security

Participants expose themselves to ridicule when they perform in front of others, especially when they are playing a role and engaging in behaviours that are unfamiliar. Brislin and Yoshida (1994) recommend that role-plays be used only after all participants, including trainees and trainers, have become comfortable with each other. For role-plays to be successful, participants must be willing to risk looking ridiculous.

Allow time for preparation

Besides being comfortable with their colleagues and trainer, participants should also have sufficient time to become comfortable with their roles by preparing and practising them before performing in front of others.

Beware of stereotyped characterisations

On the positive side, many participants enjoy exaggerating their roles, which can lighten the experience and make it fun for everyone. However, even humour can endanger the process since exaggerated behaviour can result in stereotyping, unintentional or otherwise. The danger of stereotyped behaviour is that it may reinforce previously held ideas about a cultural group and could defeat the purpose of the role-play: to explore alternative and more appropriate behaviours and not reinforce inappropriate behaviours (Van Ments, 1990).

Be aware of emotional vulnerability

One "rule" that Brislin (2000) strongly advocates is that the participants in a role-play agree not to change their parts during the actual performance once the basic events of a role-play have been worked out. Not making changes is important because problems can occur if actors are surprised by unexpected situations. Brislin (2000) explains that participants who feel threatened by a loss of control in performance may also lose control of their emotions and become upset or embarrassed. As a result, the role-playing experience can become uncomfortable for everyone and its purpose lost. McCaffery (1995) argues that role-playing may seem rather innocent or unthreatening but can actually be an emotionally overwhelming experience for some and arouse intense reactions. Thus role-plays can be an effective learning technique but should be used carefully.

The assignment

Like a traditional intercultural training programme, my intercultural communication paper uses role-playing as a learning experience for students to explore problems in intercultural interactions and to develop alternative strategies for solving problems. However, the scenario-based assessment I assign departs from the traditional scripted role-playing approach by handing the process over to the students to allow them to explore theories concerning intercultural communication problems and solutions in their own way. The brief, of course, is structured with certain requirements so that the learning objectives can be achieved but is sufficiently open-ended to give motivated students opportunities for creative exploration and play.

Students are asked to form their own teams of five or more members and create a scenario based on any settings or situations the students choose depicting the interaction of two or more cultural groups. The scenario should demonstrate how communication between two or more of the characters could fail due to their ethnocentric behaviours and attitudes. The students must also analyse the behaviours and attitudes demonstrated in their scenarios and suggest strategies for accommodating cultural differences. The scenario must then be presented again in an improved form demonstrating cultural sensitivity and tolerance. Finally, the team hands in a written copy of their script and analysis, a useful precaution since this presentation is an assessment and it is easy to omit an idea during the excitement of a performance. The time limit for each team's performance is fifteen minutes.

The teams are assessed on the following criteria: their attention to the purpose of the assignment, the organisation of their information, the creativity and originality of their scenario, their ability to work together, the quality and depth of their critical analyses and their presentation style. Each team's members receive the same grade, although there is also a participation factor that allows for some flexibility in adjusting individuals' grades based on their engagement with the preparation process. This individual participation grade derives from students' written feedback about the activity.

Attention to comfort

Brislin's caution concerning role-players' performance anxieties and emotional fragility is a significant issue and requires taking measures to consider students' well-being when assigning SBL activities, especially those that are assessments. Prior to this assignment, students received instruction concerning basic concepts of culture. Lectures, readings, tutorial discussions and exercises addressed aspects of culture such as verbal and nonverbal communication; cultural practices and traditions; chronemics or cultural perceptions of time; and differences in social behaviour.

Students also had experience as beginner ethnographers researching first-hand a culturally diverse workplace or organisation to identify and discuss the influence of cultural factors on behaviours and analyse intercultural effectiveness of management and staff. Therefore, by the time students received their scenario assignment, they had attained a degree of sophistication and facility with cultural concepts, and had had the chance to become comfortable with their classmates and teacher.

Consideration of students' comfort levels has also influenced the length of time I give them to prepare this assignment. Creativity requires time for brainstorming and crafting and the assignment schedule tries to provide for this process. For instance, students must be given time to:

* discuss, clarify and apply new and complex ideas effectively
* schedule meetings, delegate responsibilities and practise their presentations
* address the assignment, especially one that will receive a grade, thoughtfully and thoroughly.

In order to facilitate this process and avoid student frustration, I allow students at least three weeks preparation time. To date, none of the students who have completed this assignment have identified or demonstrated overwhelming fears of public performance; they have instead described the experience as "exciting" and even "fun" rather than anxiety-producing. Having enough time to develop and practise their scenario could be one reason for students' positive attitudes.

Benefits of creativity

In order for students to create the scenarios they role-play and analyse, they must draw on their own experiences or on those they may have heard about. The creative freedom afforded by the open-ended nature of this scenario assignment benefits students in a number of ways:

Relevance
Over a third of the students who usually enrol in this paper are foreign nationals, and they may have problems relating to scenarios that I develop. Instead, students can devise scenarios that are more relevant to them. Also, because these scenarios are their own, they have a sense of control over the experience and a greater level of investment in the process than if they were merely assigned a scenario to present.

Flexibility
Large classes mean there can be as many as seven teams with five to seven students in each team, and writing or locating appropriate case studies to accommodate those numbers can be difficult. However, teams can easily adjust their own scenarios to suit the structure and make-up of their groups as well as the skills of the team members.

Self-review
The process of choosing a topic requires students to review and reassess their own experiences, a skill known as self-monitoring that is essential for developing intercultural sensitivity (Chen and Starosta, 2000).

Variety and interest
Restricting the scenarios to those I provide would limit what students could explore. I could never come up with the variety of situations students have presented: e.g., the ethnocentric encounters between travellers and insensitive employees at an airport information desk; the problems experienced by new acquaintances in a bar; the misunderstandings of international business negotiators; the communication problems among culturally diverse workers at a construction site; and the high drama of parents first meeting their offspring's prospective marriage partner who is also a cultural outsider.

Not knowing what to expect makes the presentations exciting for the audience as well, and in many cases this interest seems to continue even after the performances have ended. I often videotape class performances to assess them more objectively later. Although these tapes are intended for my own use, students frequently ask to borrow them so they can see their performances. Also, former students have mentioned even a year or two later how much they enjoyed the scenario assignment. Assessments rarely provoke such positive comments and reactions.

Discovery through play

Besides having the freedom to choose their scenario situations, students also have the freedom to structure their scenes and analyses any way they wish, as long as they address all the parts of the assignment. This formal freedom results in much variety and imaginative play. One interesting outcome is that many students soon discover that the root of ethnocentrism lies in the subjective aspects of culture, in the values, norms and associations that have been learned and internalised, although the expression of ethnocentrism can be demonstrated through external behaviours and attitudes.

Representing this complex relationship between the internal and external manifestations of ethnocentrism is a problem that students have approached in a number of interesting ways. For example, many teams have had an omniscient narrator comment on the culturally specific behaviours as they take place in the dramas. Others have used title cards, or "thought bubbles", that are held up during the presentation to point out particular cultural variables being demonstrated or internal reactions to circumstances that characters are experiencing at certain moments.

Students have also integrated the required analyses into the structure of their presentation in creative ways. A number of teams, for instance, have used a television interview format with an expert commentator, such as a sportscaster or learned doctor, highlighting and explaining the ethnocentric problems as they occur in a pre-recorded 'real-life' situation. The dramas are then 'rewound' and played back demonstrating the expert's suggestions for improvements. Another team used a devil and an angel, complete with horns and wings, to represent a character's bad and good consciences and the dialogue between them as a depiction of the character's choice of ethnocentric or culturally sensitive behaviours. The use of popular and ethnic music, traditional costumes and other props adds to the impact of performances as well.

Students' feedback

Students have two opportunities to provide feedback about this assignment. The first is a questionnaire pertaining to the preparation process leading up to the presentation. Students are asked to identify their own contributions to the team activity as well as the most significant contribution of one or more of their team-mates; to provide an account of meeting times and attendance; and to rate each of their team-mates on their participation, communication, team commitment and attitude.

Students are also asked to discuss any problems that arose and how these problems were handled, and to make any other general comments they wish. Each student receives this questionnaire when the assignment is introduced and is asked to complete the form independently after the team's presentation. The purpose of this feedback is for students to have the chance to identify problems, if they had not done so during the preparation process, and to make suggestions for improving the activity.

This questionnaire also serves as an incentive to encourage students to participate since their team-mates are rating them. In addition, students have the opportunity to brag about their own and their team-mates' good work. The second feedback opportunity takes place several weeks after the assessment. This questionnaire is completed anonymously and requests that students reflect on the value of the scenario assignment as a learning experience and once again highlight any problems they may have experienced.

Generally, both feedback opportunities have resulted in similar comments. The majority of students enjoyed this assignment. A number of students commented on the novelty of the experience and described the activity, for example, as "different", "a fun way of learning" and "a good change" from the usual learning approach of reading and lecturing. This activity also seemed to strengthen the social cohesiveness of the class as well. Many of the students, especially the part-time and international students, stated they enjoyed getting to know their classmates better, making new friends and sharing ideas.

Finally, the value of the assignment as a learning activity was emphasised by most of the students, with over 75 per cent of the anonymous feedback forms describing the scenario assignment as "very" worthwhile. A number of students stated that the activity made them more interested in learning the theoretical concepts. One student who confessed to being "sceptical" about the value of the activity at first, "was surprised at the result and had fun doing it".

Problems as learning opportunities

The only problem student feedback identified concerned the actual organisation and planning of the teams themselves. One problem students had was arranging meeting times that did not conflict with various team members' classes, assignments and employment schedules. Teams usually solved this problem, however, by using other communication approaches, especially e-mail, an effective alternative to face-to-face meetings. Another problem students identified had to do with the division of labour. Although many of the students stated that their teams worked well together, others thought the work within their teams was not fairly distributed, with some students bearing more responsibilities than others. I had anticipated this problem and had developed the first feedback questionnaire to encourage student participation and alert me to any major interpersonal problems.

While not a pervasive complaint in the case of this assignment, the perception of unfairness can create tension and resentment within groups that may interfere with the success of the activity. Of course, the fact that this activity is an assessment and all team members receive the same grade makes the issue of how to reward those who take on more responsibility significant, especially to those students who are competitive and high achievers.

Rather than merely reacting to the problem by trying to "fix" it, another approach is to reconsider it within the context of the class. With this approach, the problem of working in teams can be considered in relation to the individualism/collectivism dichotomy, an important cultural variable that we cover in intercultural theory. Basically, *individualism* refers to the tendency of a culture to emphasise individual identity and rights over those of the group. Therefore, individualists value independence, competition and achievement and believe in an equitable reward system in which they are recognised for their initiative and contributions.

Collectivism refers to the tendency of people in a culture to emphasise group identity and goals over those of the individual and to link the well-being of the individual to the success and well-being of the group. Interdependence, co-operation and group harmony are more important than the recognition of individual achievement. In fact, a typical reward system for collectivists is one based on equality in which each person receives the same reward (Triandis, 1994). Often, individualists have problems working in a collectivist context, so it is not surprising that some students are distressed by a team activity that is structured according to collectivist values.

This problem can be turned into another opportunity to explore the issues of ethnocentrism and intercultural sensitivity by foregrounding the individualism/collectivism dichotomy and challenging students to address it as part of their scenario-based activity. Moreover, having students discover how to adapt to a collectivist experience can add another dimension to this assignment by giving them the chance to consider strategies for functioning in an unfamiliar context, a basic skill for intercultural communicators.

The alternative to having the students solve this problem would be to impose additional external controls to ensure that teams operate "fairly" or devise a way to grade students on their actual participation, both of which would only reinforce individualist values and would be incompatible with a collectivist activity. By making students aware of the problem as part of the assignment, they will be given the opportunity to be responsible for addressing it themselves. SBL activities are flexible enough to accommodate such adjustments in learning objectives and assignment goals without having to change the basic parameters of the task. It is just a matter of applying another "spin" to the activity and leaving it to the students, generally a creative and adaptable lot, to address. The only other requirement is for the teacher to stand back and allow the process to unfold.

Conclusion

I have discovered that SBL offers students an ideal environment within which to develop their critical skills, especially when the scenarios are the students' own creations. By drawing on their experiences, students have the chance to reconsider situations that are especially relevant to them and to explore behaviours and attitudes from a different perspective. Because the scenarios are completely their own, students invest in the learning process and seem to enjoy the challenge of understanding and applying the theoretical concepts and explaining them in their own way to their classmates.

Creative play is another valuable aspect of this assignment. Students have an opportunity for self-expression that, unfortunately, seems absent from much of their university experience. The educational benefits of having fun should not be underestimated. Finally, this scenario-based activity hands the responsibility of learning over to the students, an empowering experience that means they must draw on their own experiences and skills to learn new ideas and helps them realise that teachers are not their only learning resource. By relinquishing control in the classroom and giving students more opportunity for creativity, teachers can provide an exciting and memorable learning experience.

References

Brislin, R. (2000), *Understanding culture's influence on behaviour* (2nd ed.), New York: Harcourt College.

Brislin, R., Cushner, K., Cherrie, C. and Yong, M. (1986), *Intercultural interactions: A practical guide*, Beverly Hills, CA: Sage.

Brislin, R. and Yoshida, T. (1994), *Intercultural communication training: An introduction*, Thousand Oaks, CA: Sage.

Chen, G.M. and Starosta, W.J. (2000), 'Intercultural sensitivity', in Samovar, L. and Porter, R. (eds), *Intercultural communication: A reader* (9th ed.), Belmont, CA: Wadsworth.

Cushner, K. and Brislin, R. (1996), *Intercultural interactions: A practical guide* (2nd ed.), Thousand Oaks, CA: Sage.

Gudykunst, W. and Kim, Y. (1997), *Communicating with strangers: An approach to intercultural communication* (3rd ed.), New York: McGraw-Hill.

McCaffery, J. (1995), 'Role plays: a powerful but difficult training tool', in Fowler, S. and Mumford, M. (eds), *Intercultural sourcebook: Cross-cultural training methodologies*, Yarmouth, ME: Intercultural Press.

Mullavey-O'Byrne, C. (1994), 'Intercultural interactions in welfare work', in Brislin, R. and Yoshida, T. (eds), *Improving intercultural interactions: Modules for cross-cultural training programs*, Thousand Oaks, CA: Sage.

Triandis, H.C. (1994), *Culture and social behavior*, New York: McGraw-Hill.

Van Ments, M. (1990), *The effective use of role-play: A handbook for teachers and trainers*, New York: Kogan Page.

11

Where in the world am I? A multinational scenario

Juliana Mansvelt

Introduction

As a lecturer in human geography I am constantly trying to find ways to make links between theory and 'real life', and to encourage students to think about their own positioning in the social world. This is particularly important in my third year undergraduate paper on 'Geographies of Globalisation 'in which I explore the increasing interconnectedness between people and places through examining social, economic and political change.

The scenario discussed in this chapter has two purposes in relation to the learning objectives of the course. It is a medium for promoting active engagement with theoretical material presented in the paper and, secondly, it operates as a vehicle for students to think about the assumptions they bring to scenario decisions, assumptions which are bound in students' relative location in space and time and their own understandings of 'Where in the world am I?'

The scenario involves students assuming various positions with regard to a New Zealand firm, which is considering internationalising its production by establishing a manufacturing branch plant in another nation-state. The emphasis of the scenario is on the process as much as the product of learning. Critical to this process is an understanding of concepts of 'reflexivity 'and 'positionality' and it is to an examination of these terms that I now turn.

Reflexivity and positionality – engaging subject matters

In recent years 'post-modernity' as a condition of society and a way of seeing the world has occupied the attention of many scholars (for example: Harvey, 1989; Lyotard, 1984; Ward, 1997). As an attitude towards the world and a means of understanding it, post-modern thought has been associated with a belief in relative knowledges and a critique of universalising theories (such as Humanism or Marxism) which claim to possess the 'truth' about society and how it operates. Many postmodernists adhere to the notion of multiple and partial knowledges (i.e, that there are many knowledges both academic and 'lived', which provide different and sometimes competing ways of understanding the world). From this perspective knowledges can be seen as socially constructed and situated, that is, created as discourses in different social contexts. Discourses can be thought of as the texts (visual, aural, written) and narratives by which we understand, represent, give meaning to and structure the social world (Barnes and Duncan, 1992).

Concern with how knowledge is created and legitimised has meant concepts of reflexivity and positionality have assumed prominence in social science. Reflexivity involves a critical scrutiny of oneself as a researcher (England, 1994). It is about understanding that people are a part of, rather than separate from, the social world they seek to interpret.

There are many kinds of reflexivity (Rose, 1997; MacBeth, 2001) but most commonly the term is used to refer to recognition of the impact social science has on what we think, what is researched and how differences are seen (Tolich and Davidson, 1999). It involves assessing the ways in which values, positions and actions influence interpretations of social world. While frequently mentioned in the context of research, reflexivity has also been a focus of attention in higher education (Bleakley, 1999).

Part of understanding difference and thinking about the assumptions which underpin (powerful) theories about the social world involves reflecting on one's 'positionality'. Positionality is how a person is 'placed' or 'positioned' with regard to the subject being studied or to other participants in the process (Hay, 2000). In other words, it involves recognition of the difference one's gender, sexuality, ethnicity, age, political and religious beliefs and life experience make to how one may understand concepts and interpret or reproduce differences, (Plowman, 1995).

In my globalisation paper I am aware of my tendency to present the world 'as it is' devoid of an explicit understanding of where and how ideas and topics have been developed and the assumptions such constructions are dependent on. Self-conscious reflection by students on the assumptions and values they bring to subjects is also essential to developing a critical awareness of material presented to them and to understanding differences between their own and others' (partial) perspectives. In the sections which follow I explore how a scenario was used as a tool for learning about an aspect of globalisation and for critically reflecting on one's 'place in the world'.

Why the use of a scenario?

The scenario utilised in my Geographies of Globalisation course endeavours to encourage students to engage actively with theories of internationalisation and globalisation and to address issues of reflexivity and positionality. In the two years I have taught this course I have had a wide range of students, with approximately half to three-quarters of the class of between 24–30 students majoring in geography as part of an Arts, Science or Resources and Environmental Planning degree.

The remainder of students are drawn from a variety of disciplines and may not have taken any geography papers previously. Catering for such a range of students is challenging; consequently, I endeavour to elicit as much information and feedback as possible from the students about what they know in relation to the topics covered. The scenario provides a means of ascertaining and reinforcing the value of students' varied knowledges in the class setting.

In presenting the material on multinational development I wanted to move beyond a simple 'explain the theory and provide a concrete example' model (which I found boring) and envisaged the scenario as a way of precipitating some interest in what can be unappealing theories of multinational development. A student-evolved scenario rather than a discussion or debate appeared to be the most appropriate way of encapsulating my dual aims of learning through process and encouraging active learning in relation to theories of multinational development.

I saw the process of the scenario as a medium for encouraging students to work co-operatively to consider how their theories might be developed and the assumptions which underpinned them. By forcing the students to assume particular positions (such as a board member of a firm in favour of internationalising production, or a cabinet minister who did not want multinational development in his/her country), the scenario was intended to motivate students to think reflexively about their own positionality with regard to the issue and how this might complement/contradict the role assigned to them.

Because the process is a major part of the SBL approach, I envisaged students would learn not only the value of synthesising their own varied understandings but also the value of difference and debate in the class setting. I also hoped the exercise would highlight the difficulties implicit in such decision-making and illuminate some of the assumptions behind particular decisions (and ultimately the theories which account for these).

Where in the world am I? Setting the scenario scene

Planning

The lectures that preceded the scenario were important in setting the 'scene' for the scenario exercise. In these I focused on two themes which underpin the examination of globalisation in my paper. First, a belief that geography matters, i.e., it makes a difference to how social and economic processes are constituted and expressed – and, second, that theories or beliefs about how the world is organised are not neutral or universal but can powerfully influence how geographies are created and interpreted.

I used the example of globalisation to explain that the concept has a material basis (for example, in altering everyday experiences such as shopping in a supermarket) but that it also operates as discourses which are attached to particular individuals (subjects) and therefore position 'others' in particular ways (for example how globalisation in New Zealand since 1984 has been framed in the media and by the state as an inescapable economic imperative). I suggested that how globalisation is talked about and represented (e.g., as an economic inevitability, as an instrument of cultural homogeneity, or as multinational growth) affects how it may be interpreted and manifested in particular places. Following this discussion I gave a brief historical outline of the globalisation of the world economy and talked about the role of multinationals in globalisation processes.

Students were introduced to 'macro' rationales for globalisation of the production of commodities, that is, those reasons revolving around the need for continued accumulation of profit in capitalist society. In the lecture time immediately prior to the introduction of the scenario a case study of a multinational firm's growth and expansion was outlined. Having talked through the broader rationale for why and how firms might become multinational enterprises I introduced the scenario by asking the question "Why would an individual firm want to internationalise its production process rather than simply exporting to international destinations?" I told the students the purpose of the scenario was to answer this question, and that we would relate it back to 'formal' theories of multinational development in the next lecture and the following tutorial. The scenario was promoted as a valuable means by which their knowledges could be shared. The process of discussing and making decisions was identified as important, rather than the modelling of 'real world' behaviours or roles.

Process

A visual representation of the process of the scenario has been provided in Figure 11.1. Students were divided into two groups of approximately 12–15 students. The first group was a New Zealand firm, which exported products but was considering setting up a manufacturing branch-plant overseas. The group was asked to nominate a chief executive officer (CEO) who would moderate the discussion and provide a decision on relocation. Half the members of the firm were assigned the task of arguing against international plant expansion and were asked to compile a list of reasons why the firm should remain in New Zealand and not relocate. The other half were to assert the case for internationalisation of production and were again asked to compile a list of reasons why the firm should internationalise and provide justifications for these statements.

The second group comprised the cabinet of the government of the intended production destination of the New Zealand firm. A Prime Minister was elected by government members, who like the CEO provided all members of the cabinet with an opportunity to speak and had the 'casting vote'. Half the cabinet were in favour of the expansion of the firm, while the other half were opposed. Members on each side of the debate had to propose a list of reasons why inward investment was to be encouraged or discouraged.

All students were required to participate (to write down at least one relevant point) and to present their own position to their respective 'leader'. The class was informed that they could ask questions and obtain assistance from me at any point, and were told that they would need to make some decisions about the nature of their firm, their government, and their country during the exercise. Once the exercise began the participants soon realised that they needed to ascertain details of the firm, host and destination countries (see Figure 11.1 – involving reflections on what students needed to know).

The students debated among themselves such things as the nature of their company (size, characteristics, type of product), the nature of current and potential markets and distribution networks; the regulatory, social and economic features of host and destination countries; labour issues; and issues connected with environmental and social consequences of production on localities, and elaborated on these as the scenario developed.

Figure 11.1   The scenario process

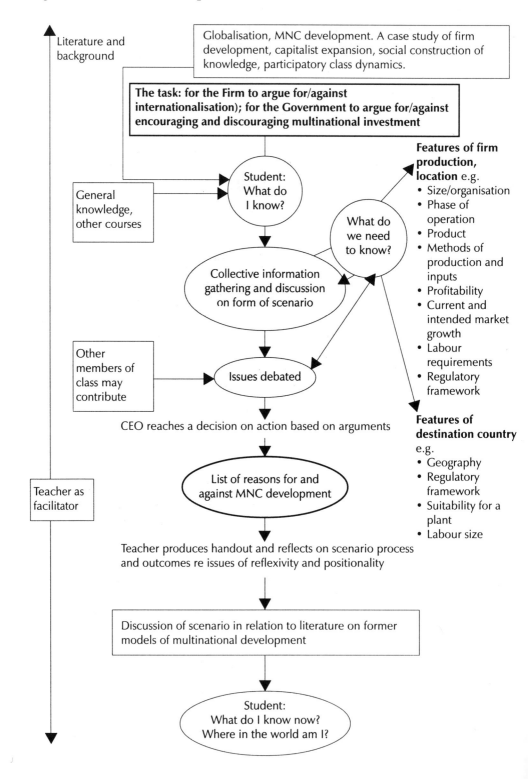

After about ten minutes I stopped the groups and we reached a collective agreement on the type of firm and its general characteristics (e.g. students chose an apparel manufacturing firm one year and a pharmaceutical company the next).

As time progressed and members began to promulgate their beliefs I found students were self-motivated to seek information to extend and incrementally create the scenario themselves. My role was as a facilitator, moving between groups and asking and answering questions to encourage participants to think about the decisions they had made, or considerations and that might make a difference to the form of their arguments. For example, when students asked me very early on what type of firm it was, I encouraged them to explain why it mattered and the difference it might make within the scenario framework.

I tried not to be too interrogative in my approach and endeavoured to motivate students to reflect on and tease out the various positions and decisions being made. My role was also to provide information, clarification and suggestions where required. I needed to be conversant with possible outcomes and implications of decisions, and making a list of potential scenario outcomes/decisions prior to the scenario would have assisted in this. Alternating between the two groups was not easy; the process would have benefited from the presence of another staff member.

Debates around relevant issues (such as whether the plant or the production process is environmentally 'friendly' or whether the destination country is a developing country or not) raised lively conversation as students could see it made the relative positions of some students easier or more difficult to argue and would affect the outcome of the exercise.

After approximately 20–25 minutes of discussion, group members were asked to present their case to the CEO and Prime Minister in front of the rest of the class (see Figure 11.1). A decision was then made whether the firm would internationalise production or not (it has always been affirmative) and whether the destination country would encourage the firm to relocate (again overall responses were always positive). The presentations of the (written) arguments were made, first by the firm to the destination government, with an opportunity for response by cabinet members both for and against the prospective relocation. This generally provoked lively debate to which any member of the class could contribute.

The entire exercise took approximately 60 minutes of a two-hour lecture slot. At the conclusion of the exercise I collected the written lists (see Figure 11.1) produced by each group and informed the group that I would collate and discuss them in relation to formal theories of multinational development in the next lecture.

Outcomes

At the conclusion of the debate I endeavoured to reinforce the value of the contributions made by each of the students to the debate. I created a one-page handout on reasons for multinational development from the written lists of scenario participants and discussed these reasons in the lecture following the scenario in relation to three formal 'academic' models of multinational development. The debriefing phase of a scenario is crucial in students' learning (Ghere, 2001) and it provided me with the opportunity to reflect on the complexity of decision-making and the issues which could be relevant to a firm's decision to internationalise. In the next lecture I talked briefly again about the exercise in relation to reflexivity and positionality. I was able to reflect (positively I hope!) on some of the assumptions held by students in delineating their positions (such as the belief that third world workers were apolitical and non-autonomous, and that developing countries were 'desperate' for inward investment) and to provide specific empirical examples.

An issue that has arisen each time the scenario has been run is the difficulty students had in reconciling moral/ethical decisions with 'business' decisions. This was an issue we were able to discuss in subsequent tutorials and lectures and which I could posit as being far more complex than an 'either profit or social justice' basis for decision-making. In retrospect I might have reflected explicitly in class on some of the difficulties I had in articulating the possible implications of decisions for scenario outcomes and on my assumptions of students' prior knowledge – both matters that demonstrate my own positionality and partial perspective!

Employing reflexivity: reflections and evaluation

There are numerous strengths and weaknesses associated with a scenario whose form is developed by the students themselves. All the students engaged in the discussion (though some more actively than others) and there was considerable laughter. A number of students rose to the occasion, treating the scenario as a role-playing exercise as well. Coming relatively early in the course (the third or fourth week), the exercise played a useful role, I believe, in facilitating class interaction and reinforcing the contribution of individuals and the collective knowledge base of the class.

The evolving nature of the scenario meant that students were forced to reflect on their assigned positions and the implications of previous assumptions (a number for example commented on the (lack of) wisdom of earlier decisions in relation to their assumed role in the scenario). Because participants in this incremental scenario approached the task from various positions and viewpoints, differences in values and perceptions were highlighted.

Further reflexivity was encouraged at the end of the exercise when we discussed as a class some of the assumptions which might lie (or have lain) behind various choices, though this introspection tended to be more 'teacher-led'. In tutorials following the lectures students commented that they enjoyed the exercise and liked the way in which the relevance of the exercise was made clear (stating that often such exercises without discussions of their relevance, are just 'time-fillers'). While some students found it difficult having to articulate positions which were at variance with their own personal standpoints and philosophies, they did feel this was a useful thing to do, something which provided insight into 'how others might see the world'.

The experiences of an overseas student in the class, who said she struggled to suggest political, social and economic factors which might prompt a New Zealand firm to relocate, provided a useful demonstration of the difference positionality can make, and challenged me about my own assumptions of class members' 'location' and the relative importance of it in relation to the scenario tasks.

It is nevertheless difficult to evaluate the success of this exercise, particularly with regard to its more esoteric aims. A more formal and extensive analysis of the scenario is needed. The scenario appeared to work better with a smaller number of 15 students (five rather than seven to eight in each subgroup) minimising the possibility of non-contributors. The class size of 20–30 students was just manageable in terms of my movement around the groups.

Undertaking the same role in a large class would prove a considerable challenge. Though two or three governments could be run in parallel without another tutor, my ability to reflect on the process would have been reduced. However, a possible advantage of more groups would have been the possibility of defining further 'types' and characteristics of governments and firms (avoiding the usual choice of a third-world nation as the destination).

I believe the assumptions made by participants about the actions of firms and governments in particular contexts are both a strength and a weakness of the scenario exercise. That 'geography' matters is a key precept of my embodiment as a geographer and so a scenario that is not grounded in anything other than the students' imaginings and discursive constructions may seem paradoxical. However, I counter this by explaining to the students before and after the exercise that the purpose of the scenario is not to model company or governmental decision-making, nor to reproduce real world contexts, but rather to think reflexively about some of the reasons why firms might choose to internationalise and the positions various 'actors' might take in relation to such a decision.

The reasons the students come up with are then discussed in relation to the academic models of firm internationalisation presented in the course text. Even though this form of 'evolving' scenario works around often stereotypical views of first and third world countries and operations of firms and multinationals (such as the association of multinational development with first world 'source' nations and third world destinations), it is still valuable as a means of trying to implode some of these notions. The scenario enabled me to highlight how varied temporal, social and geographical contexts do make a difference to the form, expression and outcome of a firm's decision to internationalise production, as well as to discuss issues of power and subjectivity which are critical to developing an awareness of positionality and reflexivity (Dowling, 2000).

Where to from here? Extensions and possibilities

In future courses I would like to build and reflect on aspects of the scenario at other points in the Geographies of Globalisation paper. In a later section of the course, I could explore the possible implications of the scenario outcome for consumption in host and destination countries, and link the scenario to other debates, for instance around trade liberalisation. The scenario itself could be expanded to incorporate a range of perspectives, such as those of firm employees in host and destination countries, and to explore outcomes such as community impacts.

I believe the scenario achieved its aims of encouraging students to engage with 'micro' rationales for the internationalisation and globalisation of production through multinational firms. Penrose (1999:227) notes that students often pay lip-service to the socially constructed nature of the categories by which we understand the world 'but then go on to work with them in ways that belie any understanding of this quality or indeed of categories in general'. Consequently, I suspect the scenario can in itself achieve little, but as part of a series of exercises it may reinforce that reflexivity and positionality are central to understanding how knowledges are created by people in particular social contexts.

Nevertheless, I believe student-centred scenarios which are not based on defined roles and prescribed answers can make a significant contribution to highlighting the openness of social systems, the contradictory and complex nature of decision-making, and the difference both place and positionality make to how processes and discourses may be constituted and acted upon. Scenarios can provide an opportunity to interrogate reflexively one's assumptions with regard to 'Where in the World am I?' and the difference one's relative place and position in time and space might make to how contexts and processes of everyday life are understood.

References:

Barnes, T. J. and Duncan, J. S. (eds) (1992), *Writing worlds. Discourse, text and metaphor in the representation of landscape*, London and New York: Routledge.

Bleakley, A. (1999), 'From reflective practice to holistic reflexivity', *Studies in Higher Education*, vol. 24, no. 3, pp. 315–331.

Dowling, R. (2000), 'Power subjectivity and ethics in qualitative research', in Hay, I. (ed.), *Qualitative research methods in human geography*, Melbourne: Oxford University Press, pp. 23–36.

England, K V. L. (1994), 'Getting personal: Reflexivity, positionality and feminist research', *Professional Geographer*, vol. 46, no. 1, pp. 80–89.

Ghere, D. L. (2001), 'Recent world crises simulations', *Teaching History*, June 2001, Issue 103, pp. 22–26.

Harvey, D. (1989), *The condition of postmodernity*, Oxford: Basil Blackwell.

Hay, I. (ed.) (2000), *Qualitative research methods in human geography*, Melbourne: Oxford University Press.

Lyotard, J. F. (1984) *The postmodern condition: A report on knowledge*, Manchester: Manchester University Press.

Macbeth, D. (2001), 'On "Reflexivity" in Qualitative Research: Two Readings, and a Third', *Qualitative Inquiry*, vol.7, no.1, pp.35–69.

Penrose, J. (1999), 'Using personal research to teach the significance of socially constructed categories', *Journal of Geography in Higher Education*, vol. 23, no. 2, pp. 227–239.

Plowman, S. (1995), 'Engaging reflexivity and positionality. Qualitative research on female single parents and residential location choice', *New Zealand Geographer*, vol. 51, no.1, pp.19–21.

Rose, G. (1997), 'Situating knowledges: Positionality, reflexivities and other tactics', *Progress in Human Geography*, vol. 21, no. 3, pp. 305–320.

Tolich, M. and Davidson, C. (1999), *Starting Fieldwork: An Introduction to Qualitative Research in New Zealand*, Melbourne: Oxford University Press.

Ward, G. (1997), *Postmodernism*, Teach Yourself Books, London: Hodder Headline.

12

Developing student-constructed scenarios to explore gender issues

Edward Peter Errington

Introduction

Several years ago, as a teacher educator within an Australian university, I employed scenario-based learning with final year trainee teachers to investigate their positions on gender issues. My use of scenarios to help students explore gender issues has been more fully documented elsewhere (Errington, 1993). For present purposes the examples described below demonstrate how scenarios can be perceived from different perspectives; from the position of the creator or storyteller; from the position of each actor within the scenario; and the position of an audience member witnessing the unfolding events. Each scenario renders a unique perspective through which students can learn about, appraise, and possibly modify their own gendered positions.

In accord with McClaren (1989), I realised as a teacher educator that students' eventual influence on promoting gender equity (as intending teachers) in schools was likely to be minimal if they were unable to articulate or critique their own perceptions of gender issues. Workers in the broader area of gender education also stress the importance of participant experiences as the fundamental starting – point for issue investigation. They echo the need to provide opportunities for students: to interrogate socially constructed events in their past (Shotter, 1984; 1986; Haug, 1987; Kippax *et al.*, 1988; Davies, 1989); to question their part within the reconstruction of gendered life stories (Haug, 1987); and to develop the ability to distance themselves from the event itself (Crawford *et al.*, 1990).

Scenario-based learning can provide opportunities for students to reconstruct and reflect on experiences and their role within them. Rather than simply discussing issues, students can adopt an active learning role – they can use their own working knowledge as the starting point for exploring, rediscovering, and evaluating personal and shared gender meanings. Scenario-based approaches which incorporate the role-playing of scenarios by students are described elsewhere (Errington, 1997).

Given the above, the purposes of this chapter are twofold: first, to describe how students as trainee teachers constructed their own scenarios to reveal and reflect on "lived" gender experiences; and second, to discuss the efficacy of this approach for facilitating multiple perspectives on gender issues.

Using student-constructed scenarios to explore gender issues

Scenario-based approaches to learning were employed with three learning objectives in mind:

- to assist participants to discover their own gender content, through the construction of relevant and authentic scenarios. It was this 'content' that needed to be worked on if students were to successfully deliver gender policies in schools. Students' own stories of sexism are more relevant than those introduced from elsewhere. It is these that trainee teachers will take with them into schools;
- to engage students in helping identify the gender positions of peers. Students were to provide each other with the motivation and support necessary for the scenario-based approach to work; and,
- to investigate the efficacy of using scenarios as a research medium. There is a desire to observe the efficacy of scenario-based approaches in order to illuminate the lived and told stories of the whole group.

My task in the following construction and representation of scenarios was to act as a resource, providing necessary impetus and support for students to assemble their "lived" gender scenarios. I was also a co-learner, intent on gaining from the richness of student stories.

Stages in the scenario-construction process

Discussion

I began the process by asking the whole group to recall particular instances where they believed they might have been the victim or perpetrator of inequities in respect of gender. It was made clear that public, not private experiences would provide the content of the discussion – that is, experiences which could be shared with others.

Sharing stories in pairs and groups

Each person was encouraged to tell their own story to a partner, and to ask questions of each other to clarify events for both teller and listener. Notably, some students simply listened and enquired about their partner's story, feeling that they had no story of their own to tell. I reminded students about the need to handle their partner's story "with care". This initial work in pairs aimed to encourage recall of gendered stories that they then could share within group settings.

Interestingly, stories were not accepted 'wholesale' by group members. Comments such as "it's not that bad surely", and "that could never happen to me", were common among males and females in respect of the expressed intensity of lived experiences.

It also became clear that recalled events were not isolated (students remembered more than one instance) and that others in the group had experienced similar events either in their personal lives (childhood, present) and/or in the professional context of schools (as trainee teachers out in schools).

Reconstructing lived gender experiences

Working in groups of five or six, group members took turns to recall lived incidents of gender inequities. I asked them to select one person's story and inquire from the selected storyteller further details of roles, events and contexts, through a process of "hot seating". Hot seating can help the storyteller remember otherwise hidden memories. Questions are asked until the essential parts of the story (the focus of the event) are remembered and understood by all members of the group. The purpose of selecting one specific, intact story, was to avoid a stereotypical (generalised) view of gender inequity.

It is the asking of questions such as: 'What did you do? How did you feel? What did the others think, feel and do? And then what happened? Why did you behave in this way?' that help to preserve the individual construction and foster group understanding of the story.

The person whose story was eventually selected was asked to direct other group members as enactors: their task would be to realise the story through the construction of a scenario. Thus, the enactors within each group were invited to question the storyteller to clarify the story, the person's part in the story and the parts played by others, and ultimately the relationships between the scenario and all those within it.

Group members were encouraged to explore how, and in what ways, the storyteller saw him/herself being positioned in relation to others as victim, specific role taker, and so on. In complementary fashion, storyteller and group participants focused on how they saw themselves positioned by significant others, such as family, friends and peers.

Once the group had chosen which story to enact, the storyteller then cast the group members to enact parts in the story. Storyteller-directors who wished to act in their own narratives were invited to do so. However, most preferred to have others enact their own (lived) roles. Some recalled later how they had felt too exposed to enact their own real-life roles in the stories.

Enacting the scenarios

When storytellers and actors had selected the particular incident or story for enactment, they then had to decide the best way that their story could be represented within a clearly defined scenario. The group worked to recreate the story of the storyteller as faithfully as possible. They were also encouraged to question the story and their responses towards it. In particular: the specific roles in the story (how these should be realised), the use of scenarios; and how these should be represented. Students also interrogated each other regarding which parts of a story should be shown, and the reasons for revealing some aspects and not others.

I continually emphasised the storyteller's ownership and how she or he should have the final say over the unfolding/final scenario and maintain fidelity to his or her own told story. Each group was given time to reconstruct the storyteller's narrative and then enact it. A number of participants decided that they would reverse gender roles.

Critically reflecting on the experience

After viewing these scenarios, the whole class gave feedback on these experiences in a number of ways. They were asked to comment on their own gender positioning in life, noting whether they had experienced similar events in the past to those experienced or witnessed here. To what extent had they felt positioned by others? How successful did they feel their own and other scenarios had been in enlivening gender as an issue? Critical reflection was encouraged within and outside the scenario. Within the scenario, participants as actors were able to comment on their perspectives; they also commented on their engagement with both the gender issue and the social relationships that appeared to influence perceptions of that issue.

Storytellers seemed to gain much by interrogating other social actors in their own gendered scenario. For example: "Why did you treat the young woman ('me' the storyteller) in that way"? It was anticipated that students as members of the audience or as non-acting storytellers were likely to relate to the scenarios, but at a distance. Similarly, actors had an opportunity to step out of the scenario, and were asked about their own responses to being in role, social relationships, and their gender incidents. They were invited then to recall their thoughts and feelings at particular stages of the whole session. This approach involves a conscious analysis and subsequent demystification of the scenario and the construction of the gendered incident.

Following a period of broader, public reflection by students as storytellers, actors and audience, all were invited to recall their immediate thoughts about the issues, the scenario, and their own positioning.

Three scenarios

Here are examples of scenarios viewed from different perspectives as storytellers, actors and/or audience.

Perspective 1: A storyteller's scenario

'Maria'[1] as storyteller, recounted her experience as a bank teller at a local bank where she worked with an inexperienced male colleague. Some months later when an opportunity arose for one teller to be promoted, preference was given to the male bank teller, regardless of his relative inexperience when compared to Maria.

Maria was actually told by her boss (confidentially of course) that because she was likely to start a family rather than pursue a long-term career in banking her promotion application had to be overlooked. This was in clear contrast to the public face of the bank manager who claimed to be an equal opportunity employer.

---

[1]   Names have been changed for anonymity.

In the scenario, Maria as storyteller decided to reverse gender roles and to take the part of the male teller herself. The inconsistent position of the bank manager, as the person directly responsible for delivering equity policies, was made clear. We saw him espouse the pride of the bank in facilitating equal opportunity for all its workers. In a later scene we see him tell Maria's immediate supervisor that "in, say, five years time she will probably be raising a family. What price then the bank's investment in management training?" According to Maria, and all other female victims, the subtext is: "You are good, but you are not good enough".

On reflection Maria recalled how she had taken the role of the male teller herself in order to give the role "a sensitive and informed treatment" (her words). She had hoped to avoid stereotyping or trivialising a significant incident in her own career/life.

Through reconstructing this lived event as a scenario, and by taking on the "oppositional" role of male bank teller herself, Maria was able to distance herself, and examine the male's point of view more dispassionately. Maria finally added that if you "go into any bank and have a look at the tellers, predominantly they're female and the people behind them are males. It might seem a generalisation, but I know it's true".

Audience reaction

Having observed Maria's story, Annie, a member of the audience, recalled a similar incident in her own life where: "there was a woman on the ground floor of the bank for ages. Finally, they just had to promote her because she'd been there for so long, but there were guys who'd been there for a shorter time who were given promotion just like that". The notion of impeded access to promotion and poor recognition of ability was common to the experiences of many female students. The majority of women in this group had at some time experienced impediments to promotion on the grounds of gender.

Perspective 2: An actor's scenario

There next followed a scenario in which two women, 'Rachel' and 'Gina', assumed roles as firefighters and rescued two males from a raging fire. On reflection, they related contrasting feelings about their common experience. The story began with Rachel asking why firefighters were predominantly male. Why, as a female, was she dissuaded from experiencing the exhilaration and empowerment afforded to male firefighters in their social role?

The enactment began at the point when the two males in their group were unable to put out a fire in their own home. We saw them being overcome by smoke inhalation. The two (female) firefighters responded quickly to a fire alarm, dashed to the rescue, and dragged the two victims from the house. The (male) victims thanked them gratefully for their courage.

Even though the scenario was simple in its execution, it gave rise to an interesting period of reflection regarding the thoughts and feelings experienced by the two females in their role as firefighters. Although working alongside each other, sharing the firefighting task, their reflections revealed totally opposite feelings about the event. It served to show that scenarios focusing on gender issues do not have to be complex to raise critical awareness.

On reflection, Rachel recalled:

> I felt a great sense of power and purpose and I wasn't worried about my appearance or what I looked like, or how I was feeling. I had a job to do and I suppose I actually felt like a *heroine* (my emphasis).

Rachel had expressed her experience in female terms as the heroine – a symbol of female power. She went on to add that she had felt a wonderful sense of purpose, responsibility, power and real worth in being a female firefighter.

On the other hand, Gina, the second firefighter, appeared uneasy with Rachel's notion of power, stating that:

> I wouldn't want to be a firefighter. I don't want to be physically strong. I don't want to have the life situation where you are dealing with other people's lives … I felt silly pulling a man out of it (fire). I felt good in a way that I could actually do it. You know I was actually pulling a man out of this and you know I am really the *hero* (my emphasis), but I still feel uncomfortable.

Thus, in contrast to Rachel, Gina framed her experience in masculine terms, implying that the archetypal hero should, and could only, be male.

Gina expressed discomfort with the role of male firefighter and did not wish to be empowered in this way. She seemed happier with clear traditional lines between female and male social roles. It is notable that Gina is more clearly positioned within a set of expectations about what male and female roles should be.

Perspective 3: audience scenario(s)

Members of the audience, watching other groups enacting stories, were often stimulated to recall similar incidents of their own, ones that appeared forgotten until now. In this sense drama provided a window to past experiences that hitherto had remained forgotten. One such enactment concerned the exploitation of males and females.

Scenario A: Males exploiting females

In 'real' life, the event focused on the exploitation of a female customer by a male garage mechanic. The recalled event involved a male mechanic and a female customer. However, in the constructed scenario, the storyteller (the real female customer) decided to reverse gender roles, that is, the exploited victim would now be male not female in the scenario, giving a twist to the lived event.

The scenario was seen by actors, audience and storyteller alike to produce mutual female/male exploitation. The (now) female mechanic exploited the male customer by making sexual advances. In return, the male customer exploited the female mechanic financially by receiving a discount for the repair.

Scenario B: Females exploiting Males

'Janis' a member of the audience recalled an incident similar to the one concerning a car mechanic and exploitation. She told us how the registration plate of her car was suspended by one side only. To get the problem fixed, she went to the garage and approached the male mechanic for help by adopting a stereotypical "dumb blonde" facade.

This ploy, where she feigned stupidity, achieved the desired result and the mechanic immediately fixed the car. Janis admitted that she exploited male assumptions about female mechanical ineptitude in order to get her way. All she had to do was to resist being her 'real' thinking self, and assume the dumb female stereotype.

The whole class considered this incident. Some males were annoyed that they (as members of the male population) were being exploited. They challenged the morality of Janis and other females who manipulated men for their own ends. Janis and others remained unrepentant, asserting that some males used similar tactics in order to get girlfriends to do (motherly) 'female' tasks such as ironing their clothes for them.

Student reflections

Overall, these reflections focused on the possibilities of change. At one end of the spectrum some students greatly resisted any notion of change, preferring clear male/female dualities and did not regard gender inequity as an issue of injustice.

Some female students registered discomfort, fearing that their femininity would be undermined if they assumed traditional aspects of maleness:

> We don't have the opportunity that men do. You know I want to be at home and look after the children. I also feel uncomfortable with it. If Scott stays home to look after them, then maybe he's taking away from me something that I might want.

Other students in the middle of this dimension of change, claimed an increased awareness of gender as an issue thanks to involvement on various levels in this scenario-based approach:

> Being the daughter who was victimised, I felt that the situation was not dealt with properly and although I was not entirely blame-free, the fact that 'boys will be boys' was not how I wished the situation to be treated (that is, I was the victim of sexism).

> What I liked about this session was looking at discrimination faced by males – something I (as a female) rarely think of. I was made more aware of discrimination against males. This discrimination does not allow men to acknowledge or partake in 'femaleness'.

Further along, more students claimed a sense of power, responsibility, and purpose, having exposed themselves to aspirations greater than those imposed by historically based male/female roles and relationships.

All claimed that the scenarios facilitated the possibility of change, regardless of some initial resistance to the exploration of gender issues:

> (When using scenarios) ... I feel that situations become more obvious as we are often looking on objectively rather than being the participant at the time. I initially could not think of examples of sexism in my life. Interestingly, as discussion began, I found I was able to empathise with several of the examples given and acknowledge similar situations myself.

A number of students shared the view that personal perceptions of gender as an "issue" have immediate implications for the professional attitudes that they will be taking into the classroom, and their ability to deliver gender equity policies.

> Gender surrounds us and permeates our lives in practically every situation. I personally am becoming more aware of: how this affects me personally; how it affects others (particularly schoolchildren); how I contribute towards sexism; and how I can remedy sexism.

As one student commented:

> It's good to actually act out roles like this because it brings our own stereotyped [sic] views and biases out in the open. I think role-playing is a challenging experience because you realise how stereotypic your own sexual differentiations are!

Rather than have persons simply replay their own gender role, some students chose to reverse positions so that they could experience the same (and often their own) story from different vantage points. So it was not unusual to see males 'being females' and vice versa. What is clear is that this convention proved to contribute greatly towards raising the consciousness and empathy of students regarding changes of positioning, and implications for 'real' life.

Some storytellers and actors decided to change the ending of the scenarios to show how they would ideally have been positioned by others in a positive way. These idealised endings did not focus on simple 'goody' moral endings; rather, they provided a fresh look at the way events might be changed en route, so that ultimately outcomes were totally different. There was clear value in students showing each other that events can take a different turn if preceding actions are enacted, deconstructed, and subsequently set on an alternative track leading to more positive outcomes.

Conclusions

Scenario-based learning provided a structure by which students, as intending teachers, were able to recount, enact and reflect on personal/social knowledge of gender construction in their own lives. Scenarios which encompassed conventions, such as role reversal and 'actual' and 'ideal' endings, and opportunities to direct one's own story proved useful in helping participants reveal and represent their lived experience.

It seems that scenario-based approaches can offer views of gender construction from a variety of roles and perspectives. Notably the simplest experiences of gender inequity provided storytellers, actors and audience with the most stimulating content for raising the level of debate. Through scenario-based approaches to learning, the previously lived stories of students can be resited within freshly experienced social contexts, and reviewed and critically interrogated from the different perspectives of actors and audience. Storytellers also valued the opportunity to view experiences "coming to life" and the chance to critically reflect on them. It is these revitalised stories and 'new' memories that students, as newly qualified teachers, will take with them into schools.

References

Crawford, J., Kippax, S., Onyx, J., Gault, U. and Benton, P. (1990), 'Women theorising their experiences of anger: A study using memory work', *Australian Psychologist*, vol. 25, no. 3, pp.333–350.

Davies, B. (1989), 'The discursive production of the male/female dualism in school settings', *Oxford Review of Education*, vol.15, no.3, pp.229–241.

Errington, E. (1993), 'Reclaiming the driver's Seat', *Education Links*, no. 46, pp. 33–36.

Errington, E. (1997), *Role-play*, Melbourne, Australia: Higher Education Research and Development Society of Australasia (Green Guide No 21 – HERDSA).

Haug, F. (1987), *Female sexualisation*, London: Verso.

Kippax, S., Crawford, J., Benton, P., Gault, U. and Noesjirwan, J. (1988), 'Constructing emotions: Weaving meaning from memories', *British Journal of Social Psychology*, vol. 27, pp.19–33.

McClaren, P. (1989), *Life in schools*, New York: Longman.

Shotter, J. (1984), *Social accountability and selfhood*, Oxford: Blackwell.

Shotter, J. (1986), 'A sense of place: Vico and the social production of social identities', *British Journal of Social Psychology*, vol. 25, pp.199–211.

Part Four

Speculative-based Scenarios

13

Writing in role: Helping students explore emotional dimensions within scenarios

Regina Pernice

Introduction

I have recently offered a new undergraduate extramural paper (by correspondence) in which I have used scenario-based learning (SBL) that includes the specialised SBL tool of 'writing in role'. The new paper is in the area of psychiatric disability, and is one of the main papers offered for both the Certificate in Rehabilitation in the Rehabilitation Programme, and the Major in Rehabilitation of the Bachelor of Health Sciences; these are taught within the School of Health Sciences at Massey University, Palmerston North, New Zealand.

The aim of this chapter is to introduce teaching colleagues to the benefits of using SBL and 'writing in role'. The latter allows assessment of how well students experience the feeling dimensions of the scenarios explored. This chapter outlines the context in which SBL/ 'writing in role' is used; the development of the scenario writing process, including the assessment criteria; the combined learning value of using SBL with 'writing in role'; and the process of evaluation. Finally, I provide some useful suggestions for colleagues who may be contemplating similar approaches themselves.

Context

As the Rehabilitation Programme in the School of Health Sciences had to date mainly emphasised physical, sensory and age-related disabilities only, it was considered necessary to also include psychiatric disability and to offer a new focus in mental health. At the time this was being discussed Schizophrenia Fellowship New Zealand (SFNZ) approached the Rehabilitation Programme to request that we offer one paper in psychiatric disability, designed specifically to help families who were struggling with problems associated with caring for people with mental illness in the community. SFNZ wanted to ensure that their staff and membership were trained in family-inclusive interventions. I offered to address this issue in the new 100-level paper in psychiatric disability. I realised the paper had to be designed to meet the needs of a large variety of undergraduate students, who could be:

- students in the rehabilitation and/or health studies programme
- part of the social work and/or psychology programme
- older students who may have been working for some years without formal qualifications in the mental health/disability area
- students who may have a family member with a severe mental illness
- students who may be mental health service users themselves.

I approached SFNZ's national liaison officer to discuss the development of the paper. Several meetings were organised in collaboration with mental health service users and their families. I contributed ideas on the academic content and asked for views on the training needed for future mental health professionals, to enable them to develop a positive and supportive relationship with families.

The responses from participants at the meetings suggested that mental health services needed to include families as 'partners in care', and therefore that training in various models of family interventions was necessary. But above all, professionals needed an understanding of the nature and experience of mental illness and how it affects all members of the family. Participants repeatedly voiced their concern that many professionals lack empathy for their situation and they ideally would have liked all professionals to have a family member with a mental illness. Acknowledging that this was unrealistic, they suggested that the acquisition of experiential knowledge should be a first priority in professional training. The exploration of emotions was considered to be of crucial importance to enable future professionals to empathise with mentally ill patients. The training would help them create a positive relationship with the family – enabling them to better assist, advise, and collaborate in the treatment process.

It became clear that the paper needed not only to offer traditional learning material (recent research articles and textbooks), but also to provide opportunities for experiential learning in order for would-be professionals (our students) to better understand severe mental illness and its effects. The following learning objectives were identified:

1. to develop empathy by understanding the nature and experience of mental illness and its effects on the family;
2. to have the ability to focus on the role of the family/whanau in mental health treatment and management; and
3. to develop knowledge of evidence-based family-inclusive interventions.

The attainment of the first objective was considered most important for success in achieving the other two. Once objective one was achieved, the other two objectives could then be met using more traditional teaching and assessment approaches. The mental health service users and their families agreed that objective one could best be achieved by using scenario-based learning as this would provide an excellent framework for experiential learning. However, the SFNZ national liaison officer suggested that it was crucial also 'to write in role' as it would take the learning process one essential step further. Students who are required to write in role would be pushed much deeper into the lives and experiences of family members in the scenario. Without the ability to put oneself in the place of the person with the mental illness, and his/her family, there may be abstract concern, but not true empathy. Therefore it was decided that SBL and 'writing in role' had to be major components of the very first written assignment of the paper that all students needed to complete to a satisfactory level.

Development of SBL and 'writing in role' as a learning tool

Students, enrolled as extramural (correspondence) students in this paper, are provided with an administration guide that includes the outline and details of the two compulsory assignments. Three study guides and two audio tapes are also provided. The first task for students is to acquire as much academic knowledge on mental illness as they can by studying the study guides, including Torrey's chapter 'The inner world of madness' (1995), from his book *Surviving schizophrenia: a manual for families, consumers and providers* (28–83). Torrey's chapter teaches students what a person with schizophrenia generally experiences if one could listen to someone with this illness. In writing this chapter Torrey relied on patients' descriptive accounts of the signs and symptoms of their illness; he also used examples from English literature. Our students are urged to read this chapter carefully.

The second task is to listen to two audio-tape recordings of mental health service users' accounts, and the experiences of their parents. Their third task is to widen their knowledge by reading some of the recommended readings. For example: the texts *Family education in mental illness* by Hatfield (1990); and *Families of the mentally ill: coping and adaptation* by Hatfield and Lefley (1987). Once students have acquired sufficient cognitive knowledge about mental illness, they are required to write their first assignment. Part 1 of the assignment (which carries 12 marks out of 20) aims to provide an experiential learning opportunity via the provision of a typical scenario. In this, the student is required to put him/herself into the shoes of another person, explore that person's feelings, sensations and experiences and record these on paper (using first person singular).

In collaboration with the national liaison officer of SFNZ, a family scenario was developed (with one member experiencing the onset of schizophrenia), that illustrates the varied emotional challenges of each person involved. It is suggested to students that they approach this task by imagining they are each individual in turn; they then focus on some of the most likely emotions, and later explain the feelings that this person might experience. The following is Part 1 of the first written assignment. Students are asked to read the following scenario carefully:

Scenario

Mere and Don have two children. Ben is ten and Julie is four. Their problems began a year ago, soon after Don was promoted to head office and the family moved to Wellington. The children began to find that they could not have fun with Dad any more. He refused to play rough-and-tumble games and he began telling them to sit still and keep quiet all the time. Mere began to notice that he was not his usual relaxed happy self: he did not laugh at her jokes any more. She soon discovered that he was often not listening to her, either. Things grew worse; Don continued to withdraw until he was seldom speaking more than an occasional word to any of them. He had always been a light sleeper, but now he was awake nearly all night. Frequent outbursts of unprovoked verbal aggression began about a month ago; never before had Don shouted at Mere and the children in that ugly fashion. Last week, he began to accuse Mere of being secretly in love with his new boss, and of trying to poison him by putting weedkiller in his coffee. Mere made an appointment to visit a GP at the local medical centre.

Once the scenario has been read, students need to retell the story from the viewpoints of each and ALL of the people mentioned. It is suggested that the task is approached in the following way:

Mere's viewpoint: Begin by trying to imagine that you are Mere. Stand in her shoes: imagine that Don is your husband and allow yourself to experience some of the most likely emotions that she may have experienced.

When the student has begun to experience some strong emotions, it is suggested that she/he begins writing as if she/he were Mere. The following instructions encourage the student to experience the emotions: Explain how you (i.e. Mere) feel about what is happening and how, at first, you attempted to explain away the changes in Don's behaviour to yourself and to the children. Tell how your fears grew as Don's behaviour deteriorated. Explain how you reacted to his withdrawal, his verbal aggression and his outrageous accusations and why now you feel compelled to seek help. (Write a maximum of three hundred (300) words from Mere's viewpoint.)

Ben's viewpoint: Begin by trying to imagine that you are Ben. Think back to the things you did with your own father when you were ten years old. Imagine that Don is your father and that he has stopped doing those things with you. How do you feel?

When you have begun to experience some strong emotions, begin writing as if you are Ben. Explain your (i.e. Ben's) emotions. (Write a maximum of fifty (50) words from Ben's viewpoint.)

Julie's viewpoint: Begin by trying to imagine that you are Julie. How do four-year-olds feel when they are pushed away by people they love? Can they sit still and remain quiet for long periods?

When you have begun to experience some strong, childish emotions, begin writing as if you are Julie. Explain how you have been responding to your father's hurtful behaviour. (Write a maximum of fifty (50) words from Julie's viewpoint.)

Don's viewpoint: Begin by carefully studying 'The inner world of madness' (Torrey's book chapter in Study Guide One). As you read, note any symptoms that might explain Don's change in behaviour. Look for clues that will help you to understand some of the most likely emotions people experience (according to 'The inner world of madness') when they are developing a serious mental illness, then imagine you are Don.

When you have begun to experience some strong emotions, begin writing as if you are Don. Describe your emotions, the strange new sensations and problems you are experiencing and the delusional beliefs you have constructed to explain your new sensations and problems. (Write a maximum of five hundred (500) words from Don's viewpoint.)

Doctor's viewpoint: Begin by imagining that you are a GP. Your waiting room is full, you have had to work right through your lunch hour. You have not been trained to understand the way families react when a member begins to appear mentally unwell. Mere has booked a ten-minute appointment with you. When she enters your room, she bursts into tears, raves on about how difficult her husband is to live with, and keeps repeating "It is not true, doctor, I am not having an affair with his boss." What do you decide the problem must be? How do you feel when Mere does not want to leave when you signal that she has overstayed her ten-minute appointment?

When you have begun to experience some strong emotions, begin writing as if you are Mere's doctor. Describe the emotions, state your diagnosis of the problem and explain how you try to help Mere. (Write a maximum of one hundred (100) words from the doctor's viewpoint.)

Assessment of Part 1 (Assignment 1)

Part 1 of this written assignment is assessed and graded on how well the student is able to describe the emotional content of the individual's experience; the student can receive 12 marks out of 20 for this part. In order to evaluate this approach I developed a set of expectations or standards. These expectations (criteria) have been formalised in an assignment marking sheet, as follows:

Mere's viewpoint:

Focus on emotions throughout (1 mark)
Evidence of likelihood of an escalation of emotions (1 mark)
Evidence of the likelihood of widespread effects of Don's illness on the family (1 mark)

Possible Mark	Your Mark	Comments
3		

Ben's viewpoint:

Focus on direct emotions throughout (1 mark)
Evidence of the likelihood of widespread effects of Dad's illness on 10-year-old Ben (1 mark)

Possible Mark	Your Mark	Comments
2		

Julie's viewpoint:

Focus on childish emotions throughout (1 mark)
Evidence of the likelihood of widespread effects of Dad's illness on four-year-old Julie (1 mark)

Possible Mark	Your Mark	Comments
2		

Don's viewpoint:

Focus on emotions throughout (1mark)
Evidence of likelihood of Don experiencing at least four abnormalities (see Torrey's chapter 'The Inner World of Madness')

Possible Mark	Your Mark	Comments
3		

Doctor's viewpoint:

Focus on emotions throughout (1 mark)
Evidence of diagnosis and treatment for Mere (1 mark)

Possible Mark	Your Mark	Comments
2		

Some students telephoned at the time they wrote their assignments; I encouraged them to follow the guidelines closely. When I return the marked assignments I provide extensive feedback to all students, and particularly for those few who experience particular difficulties with Part 1 of Assignment 1. I like to make sure that they can progress to the academic part of the paper.

The learning value of using SBL and 'writing in role'

As mentioned before, the scenario provides a good framework for experiential learning. However, 'writing in role' is the crucial exercise for students to meet Objective 1 of the paper. The task of exploring and experiencing the feelings of each individual family member, as if they really were that person themselves, and the recording of this experience provides some deep and essential insights.

Given the above scenario, students (in the role of MERE) wrote about her confusion about Don's shouting at her and the children, and her initial explanation that he was stressed by his new job. Students described a wide range of escalating feelings. One student in the role of Mere wrote:

Then he withdrew and at first I was furious when he was just sitting there, shrinking inside himself, closing himself off to us, ignoring us. But then it started to feel creepy and he stayed up all night, pacing up and down the room and I felt scared, really scared and worried about what is going to happen next. I could not sleep any more and I felt exhausted and then things became even worse. He accused me of having an affair with his boss. I was outraged and I felt hurt that he had no trust in me any more and we had horrible scenes. I feel everything around me overwhelming me and falling to pieces. A few days ago he stopped eating anything I had touched or cooked and he accused me of trying to poison him to get rid of him. I am horrified, I don't understand, it is a never-ending nightmare. I feel so desperate.

A student, writing in the role of BEN, said: *I am angry with Dad, I hate him, I hate his new job and I hate Wellington. I feel like running away, he just rants and raves all the time.* Some students felt shame and embarrassment about Dad and stopped inviting friends home. Sometimes anger against Mum and feelings of regret that Dad had stopped playing with Ben and his sister were also expressed.

JULIE was described as afraid, bewildered, disturbed and lonely. For example a student wrote: *I hide when Daddy comes home, he shouts at me all the time and I am scared. He does not read stories to me any more. Daddy does not love me any more.* Some students expressed Julie's feeling that the loss of Dad's love was somehow her fault.

The role of DON presented difficulties for some students. They experienced him as a man stressed by relocation and by increased work pressures, rather than a man who was getting mentally unwell. However, those students who had carefully read Torrey's chapter 'The inner world of madness' were able to enter the role deeply enough and to describe Don's isolation, his sleepless and restless nights; they could also empathise with his torment, and the horror and fear of the delusions and hallucinations that created enormous suffering. Some students in Don's role focused on obsessive jealousy and paranoia about Mere's affair with the boss which led to intense fear of being poisoned by Mere. As one student put it:

I watched from the window and I saw her phoning her lover on the mobile. I knew it, the bloody bitch, she walked sneakily to the garage and got the weedkiller. When she returned and saw me sitting there she was so keen to make me a cup of coffee. I was horrified, I yelled and screamed at her that she and the kids were plotting against me and trying to get rid of me. I am terrified, terrified of anything she touches or cooks.

In the role of the DOCTOR students had many ideas about a possible diagnosis of Mere's state of mind; these ranged from her suffering premenstrual tension (PMT), marriage problems, depression, or an anxiety disorder, to a diagnosis of stress due to relocation. As a consequence of these perceptions, treatment focused on counselling for Mere, or marriage guidance counselling, the prescription of anti-depressants or anti-anxiety medication. Few students were able to focus on the doctor's feelings, such as being overwhelmed by an unmanageable workload and therefore feeling irritable and annoyed, or feeling hungry (no lunch break) and tired.

As the above examples demonstrate, the use of a family scenario where one member of the family experiences mental illness, and where students are required 'to write in role' to focus on emotions, has a number of educational benefits for students:

- *Awareness is raised of the interconnectedness of feelings, thoughts and behaviours, and their effect on physical health.* (For example, in the role of Mere, students talked about having *feelings* of distress; these were accompanied by *thoughts* of possible danger, and these led to increased vigilance and sleeplessness *(behaviour)*, resulting in physical exhaustion that could lead to physical and emotional neglect of both herself and the children.)
- *Awareness is raised of the multiple emotions that could rapidly escalate in intensity.* (For example, Don's escalation of emotions from fear and suspicion to terror, horror and obsessive paranoia.)
- *Awareness is raised that children as young as Ben and Julie are severely affected by mental illness.* (For example, Ben's and Julie's total incomprehension, fear, anger, shame and feelings of loss, guilt and self-blame.)
- *Awareness is raised of the emotional dimensions of health professionals.* (For example, the doctor's feelings of being overworked and overwhelmed.)
- *Awareness is raised of the various service needs of this family in crisis in order to prevent its total disintegration.* (For example, students realised that Mere and the children needed support, information and education about mental illness. This could enable Mere to support Don's assessment and possible short-term hospitalisation and treatment.)

Overall, in the light of their experiences of writing in role, students were now ready to learn more about family-inclusive interventions and the need for treatment models.

Process of evaluation

When the paper was offered for the first time, I invited students to provide feedback so I could modify the assignment topics and/or the study guide materials for future offerings. The evaluation form included in the administration guide was returned by most students. I also received a large number of telephone calls that provided useful oral feedback on the paper.

Students' feedback singled out Part 1 of Assignment 1 as being the most important and most stimulating exercise of the whole paper. Their written and/or oral comments made clear that 'writing in role' not only illuminated their understanding of the emotional dimensions of the experience, but also revealed the actual service needs of the various individuals. Students described their growing awareness as "a light bulb being switched on" or stated that "the penny dropped". Some students reported that they too had experienced mental illness in the past, and had some difficulty putting themselves in the shoes of another family member. However, they generally persevered with the task and commented, via the evaluation form, that they had benefited from the exercise. One student mentioned how he now felt more sympathy for his parents.

'Writing in role' was less successful with those students who had a family member with mental illness; they felt it brought up too many painful feelings of the suffering experienced at the time. They commented on how they could have done without this exercise, presumably because they had already learned its lessons.

Suggestions for colleagues wishing to use SBL and 'writing in role'

SBL and 'writing in role' can be used in training with similar discipline areas that have a large interpersonal component in service provision, for example, professionals in mental health, health education, nursing and social services. The advice to colleagues who may want to adopt an experiential learning approach is to realise the importance of considering what end-users (clients, patients and/or mental health service users and their families) want from the professionals you are trying to educate.

The scenario in this particular assignment could be modified; for example, by having a teenager – perhaps in a family with older and younger siblings, who experiences mental illness. In addition to learning about the emotions of the person with the illness, students would have opportunities to explore the experience and feelings of the parents and (most importantly) the siblings in an in-depth way. Another possible scenario could explore the experience of a first-year university student becoming unwell. Using writing in role, students could explore the emotions and experience of the student, his/her friend, the hostel manager, the older sibling (who is at the same university and follows an advanced course of study) and the parents who live far away.

For students studying on campus, I would follow up the writing-in-role task by facilitating role-play exercises. Role-playing can reveal similar insights into the experiences of service recipients. One advantage of writing in role is that students don't experience the possible embarrassment and/or discomfort of having to role-play in front of fellow students. It may be difficult to make participation in role-play compulsory, and therefore it may be less effective as a learning/assessment tool for *all* students.

Conclusion

SBL and writing in role have been extremely valuable teaching methods for meeting the number one objective of the paper, namely to develop empathy by understanding the nature and experience of mental illness and its effects on all family members. It has proven to be an excellent learning tool for most students as demonstrated by the most positive evaluations of this paper. In particular, writing in role provided essential opportunities for experiential learning by ensuring that students explored the emotional dimensions and their effects from the perspective of each family member. This task clearly enhanced students' awareness and understanding of both the complexity of the issues involved when caring for families in crisis, and the intervention and service needs of families. In-depth understanding of the nature and experience of mental illness and its effects on the family also facilitated the subsequent academic (cognitive) learning process as it relates to various models of successful family-inclusive interventions.

References
Errington, E. (1997), *Role-play*, Melbourne, Australia: HERDSA Publications.

Hatfield, A. B. (1990), *Family education in mental illness*, New York: Guilford Press.

Hatfield, A. B. and Lefley, H. P. (1987), *Families of the mentally ill: Coping and adaptation*, New York: Guilford Press.

Torrey, E. F. (1995), *Surviving schizophrenia: A manual for families, consumers and providers* (3rd ed.), New York: Harper Perennial.

14

Living forever? Exploring mortality and immortality with scenario-based learning

Mary Murray

Introduction

Until very recently the death of our physical bodies has been the only certainty in life and one that lies at the heart of human experience. Despite this, in many contemporary Western societies there is a marked reluctance to come into contact with the dying and the dead. This could be an expression of what Becker (1973) considers a universal fear of death that is intrinsic to the human condition. This fear may have been accentuated in Western societies by the separation of the dying and the dead from the living in hospitals, hospices and rest homes (Aries, 1974; Elias, 1985). Meanwhile the medicalisation of death has constructed death as a failure, either on the part of the medical profession or on the part of the dying person, rather than as a natural biological process and also, perhaps, as a rite of passage offering opportunities for spiritual transformation – of the religious or humanistic kind.

Surprisingly, sociologists have not been particularly interested in death. Partly as an attempt to address this lacuna, for the last few years I have been teaching a paper about death and dying. Though based within a sociology programme, given the centrality of mortality to human experience the paper draws on a wide range of disciplines within the social sciences and humanities. The popularity of the paper is, I believe, partly related to its subject matter: sooner or later each and every one of us will come face to face with, and may try to make sense of, our own mortality as well as the mortality of others, especially those we love.

Another factor contributing to the popularity of the paper is, I believe, related to some of the teaching methods employed within the course, one of which is scenario-based-learning, used alongside more conventional approaches. The choice of a scenario-based learning method was influenced by educational objectives within the course. One of the key educational objectives is that of increasing awareness of the social dimensions and implications of mortality. Rather than viewing death solely as a biological and/or spiritual phenomenon, the course considers ways in which society and social institutions shape and are shaped by death. Another objective is that of increasing awareness about mortality with a view to encouraging fuller and richer living.

I could have tried to meet these educational objectives by relying on conventional teaching methods such as lectures and tutorial discussion. However, such methods don't always engage the whole person. Conventional teaching methods certainly encourage the acquisition of theoretical knowledge and the development of analytical reasoning. But this is often at the expense of experiential, intuitive and affective dimensions of learning and knowledge-making. To meet educational objectives within the course – 'bringing to life' the social and personal dimensions of death – I needed to use a method that could tap into emotional, sensory and intuitive experience and awareness, encouraging creativity and imagination.

Before I started to teach the paper on death and dying I had developed an interest in the work of Constantine Stanislavski (1980a, 1980b, 1980c) and Lee Strasberg, (1989) both of whom have had an enormous influence on the development of acting. 'Method Acting' as developed by both these actor-directors encourages an actor to tap into their own emotional experience when playing the role of any particular character. Where an actor is playing the role of, for example, a grieving spouse, they are encouraged to tap into their own emotional memory of grief and loss to bring greater depth of feeling and authenticity to the role.

I had also discovered the psycho-dramatic work of Moreno (1987). As a psychotherapist Moreno's approach to healing was to get people to enact different roles within themselves as well as those adopted by others with whom they had a relationship – e.g. friend, child, parent, spouse, employer etc. Moreno's intention was to put people more in touch with their emotional experience, integrating it into awareness. With the clearer understanding of ourselves that may emerge from this process we may be able to make changes in our lives, should we wish to do so. I had also had some experience of scenario-based learning and the technique of role-play within higher and community education, and as a student of counselling and psychotherapy. All of this encouraged me to believe that scenario-based learning might provide the kind of educational experience needed to fulfil educational objectives within the course, central to which is a view of death as part of life and therefore 'lived' experience.

In this chapter, I outline one of the ways in which I use scenario-based learning in a tertiary level sociology course about death and dying. I focus on the way in which scenario-based learning enables me to meet educational objectives within the course and provide practical information about the planning and delivery of the particular scenario discussed in this chapter. I then spend some time outlining the scenario. To do this I trace the way in which I 'set the scene' for students by providing some mythological accounts of the origins of death and some consideration of the way in which the human desire for immortality has been expressed in both mythology and science. A detailed consideration of how I present the scenario about immortality to students follows. This is accompanied by a detailed discussion of the way in which the scenario encourages students to explore issues surrounding mortality and immortality. It is my hope that readers will find the chapter interesting and enjoyable and that it might provide sufficient stimulation to encourage the use of scenario-based learning in other educational contexts.

Planning and delivery of the session

Having decided upon the use of scenario-based learning at the very beginning of the course I find that paying attention to the classroom environment and making sure that I know at least a little about students enrolled for the course is both helpful and important for the overall success of the session.

'Round robin'

- Introduces the tutor and students to each other – interests, backgrounds, abilities, life experience – including bereavement, reasons for doing the course.
- Signals to the tutor social and personal experiences students can draw upon for the development of the scenario.
- Enables the tutor to monitor emotional safety, particularly where the students have experienced bereavement.

Classroom environment and ambience

- A large seminar room rather than lecture theatre provides degree of warmth and intimacy and contributes to an atmosphere of emotional 'containment'.
- Limited use of physical space can encourage exploration of the 'inner space' of creativity and imagination.
- The humour and sense of fun that emerges naturally provides a lighthearted touch that contributes to an overall sense of safety and support.

There now follows an outline and discussion of the scenario, explored in two parts:

Setting the scene

The origins of death: Mythological accounts

I begin by explaining to students that every culture has a myth about how death entered the world. In most mythological accounts death did not exist when human beings were created. However, death entered the world when humans disobeyed God. As the ancient Greeks saw it, an act of transgression by Pandora brought death into the world (Bulfinch, 1981: 38–42). According to the Greeks, Pandora was the first woman created after man. The Gods gave Pandora a casket sealed by them and told her not to open it. Overcome by curiosity, however, Pandora and her lover Epimethus opened the casket and released all manner of evil and misfortune into the world, including sickness, strife, grief and death. Realising their terrible and tragic mistake Pandora and Epimethus slammed the casket lid down. Although they were too late to keep the evils from escaping, they managed to trap hope inside the casket. According to the ancient Greeks this explains why we die and why, despite the existence of evil and death, the whisper of hope inside Pandora's box remains with us.

The biblical story of Adam and Eve in the Garden of Eden contains many of the elements of the story of Pandora. After God had created Adam as the first man he created the first woman – Eve – from Adam's body to be Adam's companion and helpmate. God told Adam and Eve that they could eat any fruit that grew in the Garden of Eden except fruit from the tree of knowledge. Tempted, however, by a serpent (which in pre-Christian religion was a symbol of immortality) to eat fruit from the tree of knowledge, Eve, the mother of all the living, became a carrier of death. Eve encouraged Adam to eat the fruit and, having acquired knowledge of good and evil, both of them were thrown out of the Garden of Eden and exposed to every kind of suffering, including death.

The quest for immortality in mythology and science

Long before the legend of Pandora and the biblical story of Adam and Eve, however, human beings desired immortality. This desire is expressed in what may be the first story ever written. The Epic of Gilgamesh was handed down the generations through the oral tradition of storytelling, eventually being recorded in written form in the script developed by the Sumerians – over three thousand years before the birth of Christ. In this story, stricken by grief following the death of his friend Enkidu, the hero-king Gilgamesh searches for the secret of immortality. Despite being part god and part human, Gilgamesh is defeated in his quest and dies a mortal's death (Bryson, 1st ed.).

The quest for immortality is also expressed in the Maori myth of Maui and the Death Goddess. Maui's mother had prophesied that her son would live forever. This encouraged Maui to believe that death was simply another adversary to outwit and he would not listen to his father's protestations to the contrary (when Maui was baptised his father forgot to include a passage of the incantation, thereby undoing the prophecy). This meant that Maui was destined to die like other human beings at the hand of the goddess of death Hinenuitepo – the Great Mother of the Night. Unwilling to believe his father, Maui shared his scheme for defeating the goddess and death with the fantails and set off with them to find the sleeping goddess. Maui's scheme was to enter and pass through Hinenuitepo's body, coming out through her mouth. Tragically, however, the goddess was awoken by the laughter of the fantails. She immediately closed her thighs on Maui, breaking his body into two. Because of Maui's failure human beings continue to die (Greene and Sharman-Burke, 1999: 266–277).

Though scientific knowledge is sometimes drawn upon to repudiate beliefs about life after death, scientific knowledge may yet provide a key to immortality. Today the quest for immortality and the death and rebirth archetype that often accompanies this quest are present in scientific endeavour. The Pharaohs of ancient Egypt were embalmed and entombed in the belief that their bodies would be preserved for life after death. In present-day USA the practice of cryogenics carries a similar intention: dead bodies, are frozen in liquid nitrogen in the hope that science may at some future date come up with a cure for the illnesses that killed them, so that they can then be revived and live again. There have been stories of people who have chosen to have only their heads frozen, presumably in the hope that at some future date their head can be attached to a healthy new body. At this point, I like to show a very short video clip from the last television drama written by the late British playwright Dennis Potter. 'Cold Lazarus' is a science-fiction thriller in which a human head is kept alive by machinery. The image of this futuristic cyborg is startling and moving and was chosen to show to students because of the way in which it seems to ignite an imaginative and emotional response on the part of the viewer.

More recently, following the cloning of Dolly the sheep, human reproductive cloning, once only a science-fiction scenario explored in films such as *The Boys from Brazil*, has become technically possible even though ethically controversial. Whilst many people no longer believe in the supernatural or subscribe to the belief that human beings have souls, by creating an exact genetic replica of one parent, human reproductive cloning offers the possibility of 'immortalising our genetic selves' (Somerville, 2000:55–88). Meanwhile, Japanese researchers have apparently discovered a gene that appears to suppress ageing. They have called the gene *klotho* after the Greek goddess who spins the thread of life (Bova, 1998:71). Indeed the Human Genome Project would seem to suggest that, paraphrasing Shakespeare, '... the key to immortality is not in the stars but in our genes' (Bova, 1998:107). With a complete map of our genes we may learn how to protect and repair genes involved in life-threatening illnesses. Eventually we may find out how to reset our cellular clocks and extend the span of human life indefinitely (Bova, 1998:107).

Having provided students with a mythological and scientific backdrop aimed at encouraging imaginative thinking, I then present a scenario to them, which they are invited to explore.

Conversations with our immortal selves: A dialogue about scenario-based learning

Students are invited to imagine that they live at some point in the future when scientific developments have found a way of enabling humans to live forever: humans are now potentially immortal, though not indestructible. Although we no longer die from natural causes, we can die as a result of execution, suicide, euthanasia, murder and accident. Students decide for themselves whether or not an ageing process accompanies immortality.

The group is then divided into pairs and allocated roles within dyads. One of the educational objectives of the course is the development of an understanding of the social implications of mortality. Just as death is a biological process and, for many people, a rite of passage offering the possibility of spiritual transcendence, the fact of our mortality also impacts upon and shapes the myriad of social relationships and social institutions that make up society. The choice of dyads is to some extent determined by the students themselves and what I have learnt about them and their experience from the introductory 'round robin': I am usually able to gauge what will be feasible in terms of their experience, and what it may be advisable to avoid – for example, if a member of the group has only very recently lost a parent, then it is probably not a good idea to allocate them to a dyad of child and parent.

The dyads that usually emerge from the collective experience of the group include parent/child; spouse/spouse; sibling/sibling; student/teacher; employee/employer; doctor/patient; politician/elector and religious person/atheist. Students are encouraged to draw upon their own experience and relationships in role when exploring ways in which immortality might impact upon the relationship of the particular dyad that they are exploring. I allocate about 15 minutes for this exploration, during which my own role is that of participant observer, moving between dyads encouraging students to explore implications of immortality within their particular role.

In the ensuing plenary session of about half an hour students are asked to reflect upon and report back to the group as a whole what issues emerged from within their roles. The discussion that follows usually provokes a good deal of debate and exploration within which my role is that of participant as well as recorder of key ideas and issues, relating them to educational objectives. Ideas and issues that emerge often involve an exploration of the positive and negative implications of immortality for particular social roles and relationships, all of which entails a degree of imaginative speculation on the part of group members. One of the positive aspects of immortality that is frequently identified by students is that of sparing us the pain of grief that accompanies the death of a loved one.

The possibility that our time spent in any particular relationship may not after all be rendered finite by death is also frequently seen in positive terms – the passage of time could help relationships become richer, deeper and more intimate. As individuals we may also become richer and deeper in terms of our emotional experience, knowledge and wisdom. Immortality might allow us to have numerous occupations and careers, enabling us to develop all of our talents and interests. The possibility of key historical figures such as Gandhi, Martin Luther King, Jesus Christ, and the Dalai Lama never dying is often seen in highly positive terms in so far as it could contribute to the eradication of suffering in the world.

More pessimistically, students sometimes imagine the horrors of a world in which figures such as Hitler, Stalin, Mussolini or Genghis Khan never died. Students often suggest that society may become more secular because fear of death as one basis for religious belief might disappear. The absence of religious faith in the context of endless existence might also provoke a crisis of meaninglessness. Meanwhile, whether or not they agreed, the medical profession might be increasingly called upon to assist people to die. Students sometimes argue that euthanasia might become more acceptable as a way of trying to deal with increasing overpopulation. We may also become so bored and fed up with living forever that, particularly if we are also subject to the infirmities of old age, death could become an attractive prospect: more requests for euthanasia as well as increased suicide rates might emerge. At this point I sometimes show the final painful scene in Dennis Potter's *Cold Lazarus* in which the futuristic cyborg – the head severed from its body and kept alive by a machine – pleads to be allowed to die.

Immortality could also have a dramatic influence on family life. The marriage vow of 'till death us do part' may undergo an even more radical re-evaluation than it has in the last few decades in Western societies. Serial monogamy could become firmly established as the expected norm, and, especially if fertility keeps pace with immortality, the 'blended extended' family might replace the nuclear family as the norm and the ideal. Inheritance practices and laws of succession might also be subject to radical revision or Prince Charles really might not ever be king. Moreover, if the new gene technology was only available to certain sections of the population, i.e. those who could afford it, immortality might perpetuate privilege and accentuate social inequality and divisions between rich and poor.

An important function of the plenary session is that of relating the discussion to course objectives, one of which is that of increasing awareness of the social implications of mortality. The depth and creativity of the discussion that usually unfolds in the plenary session is a good indicator that students have been able to make these linkages and my contribution in this context becomes that of attempting to deepen perception of these linkages and suggesting possibilities that may not have occurred to them.

Another important objective within the course is that of increasing awareness about the finitude of our lives in the hope that such awareness might encourage us to lead fuller and richer lives. With this in mind, towards the end of the plenary session I ask students whether, in the light of our exploration and discussion thus far, they feel that they would like to live forever. The response to this question usually hinges around meaning and purpose in life. Many students seem to feel that the fact that we are mortal is more likely to provoke us to use our lives in a purposeful way than might be the case if we were faced with the prospect of immortality: it is the finitude of embodied life that motivates the quest for purpose and meaning. On the other hand, immortality might provide us with the time to ensure that we did create and live lives infused with purpose and meaning.

Whether mortality or immortality is the preferred choice, students invariably perceive that a sense of meaning and purpose is of crucial existential significance in enabling us to lead fulfilling lives. At this point I sometimes suggest to students that our fear of death may be more acute if we feel that we have not fully lived: put another way, fear of death may actually tell us something about fear of living. If appropriate I also make reference to the work of the renowned psychiatrist Victor Frankl in his book *Man's Search For Meaning* (1984). Frankl spent several years in a Nazi concentration camp, during which time he observed that those people more likely to survive the horrors of the concentration camps were those who were able to move beyond despair and find some meaning in their experience. It was his own experience and that of his fellow prisoners in the concentration camp that led Frankl to conclude that 'Man's search for meaning is the primary motivation in his life' (Frankl, 1984:121).

Conclusions

Whilst the course as a whole has been evaluated through the quality assurance system at Massey University, the results of which have been very positive, this particular scenario approach was not singled out for evaluation. Thus far I have relied upon informal evaluation on the part of students and myself. On the basis of this I am confident that the method has made a positive contribution to meeting particular educational objectives within the course. The creative and imaginative thinking that emerges from the role-play demonstrates that students begin to perceive the social implications of mortality. By opening up this area right at the beginning of the course my intention is to provide sufficient stimulation to inspire them to continue thinking about the issue as the course progresses. The willingness of students to begin to explore and voice their imaginative and emotional responses to the prospect of immortality also opens up the issue of meaning and purpose in life and can remind us of the importance of leading lives that we find fulfilling.

Even so, there is room for development and improvement. In some ways limitations of time (about an hour and a half) and space, together with my limited knowledge of students at the beginning of the course, work against the feasibility of opting for more-developed scenarios. However, the success of the particular scenario outlined here has encouraged me to think about how more-developed scenarios might be utilised later on in the course. A number of possibilities might work, one of which is that of constructing a debate. Set against the backdrop of a scenario of human immortality, students would be invited to explore ethical issues surrounding euthanasia and assisted suicide. Divided into two groups representing two major political parties sitting in Parliament, one of whom was in favour of euthanasia and assisted suicide whilst the other was against, students could explore and debate the topic, during which time my role would be that of facilitator, chairperson, and sometimes devil's advocate.

The intention of getting students to debate such an ethical minefield in this particular way (presently the issues are explored using different methods) would be to highlight ways in which societal norms and expectations as well as issues of meaning and purpose are embedded in ethical issues surrounding death. Another approach could be that of combining certain dyads to meet specific educational objectives. For example, combining the dyads of doctor/patient, religious person/atheist, and student/teacher into one group and asking students to construct two very brief scenes exploring the scenario of immortality could enable deeper exploration of meaning and purpose. Similarly, by combining the dyads of spouse/spouse, sibling/sibling and, say, grandmother/ grandfather, again asking students to construct two brief scenes exploring the scenario of immortality, the social implications of mortality – in this case with reference to the family – could be further investigated. My hope is that future development of scenario-based learning will be as well-received by students as the particular scenario discussed in this chapter has been.

More generally, I am increasingly convinced that students more readily engage with and derive more benefit from academic work that encourages their imagination and emotional connection to the world of the intellect. Scenario-based learning can facilitate these kinds of connections and as such provides a significant resource for learning, critical thinking and knowledge-making.

References

Aries, P. (1974), *Western attitudes towards death*, London: Marion Boyars.

Becker, E. (1973), *The denial of death*, New York: Free Press.

Bova, B. (1998), *Immortality: How science is extending your life span and changing the world*, New York: Avon Books.

Bryson, B. (1st ed.), *Ginghams*, Canada: Holt, Rinehart and Winston.

Bulfinch, T. (1981), *Myths of Greece and Rome*, Middlesex: Penguin.

Elias, N. (1985), *The loneliness of the dying*, Oxford: Blackwell.

Frankl, V. (1984), *Man's search for meaning*, New York: Simon & Schuster.

Greene, L. and Sharman-Burke, J. (1999), *The mythic journey: The meaning of myth as a guide for life*, Sydney: Simon & Schuster.

Moreno, J. (1987), *The essential Moreno. Writings on psychodrama, group method and spontaneity* (2000), (Ed.) Fox, J., New York: Springer.

Somerville, M. (2000), 'The ethical canary: Science, society, and the human spirit', London: Penguin.

Stanislavski, C. (1980), (a) *An actor prepares*, (b) *Building a character*, (c) *Creating a role*, London: Methuen.

Strasberg, L. (1987), *A dream of passion: The development of the method*, London: Methuen.

Acknowledgements

I would like to thank students for their contribution to and participation in the course, all of which continues to stimulate me to work in the area. Thanks also to Stuart Hubbard for suggesting relevant movies and listening to my ideas and Ed Errington for encouragement and editorial suggestions. Paul Winstanley originally suggested that I ask students if they would like to live forever. Paul died suddenly on New Year's Day 2002.

Index

List of contributors

Stephen Bell
Senior Lecturer, Environmental Health
Institute of Food, Nutrition and Human
    Health
Massey University
New Zealand
e-mail: S.J.Bell@massey.ac.nz

Judith Bernanke
Lecturer in Communication
Department of Communication and
    Journalism
Massey University
New Zealand
e-mail: J.Bernanke@massey.ac.nz

Susan Brock
Senior Lecturer, School of Health
University of Wolverhampton
United Kingdom
S.brock@wlv.ac.uk

Angela Darvill
Senior Lecturer, School of Nursing
The University of Salford
United Kingdom
e-mail: A.Darvill@salford.ac.uk

Dr Edward Peter Errington
Training Development Unit
Massey University
New Zealand
e-mail: E.P.Errington@massey.ac.nz

Sandra Gammer
Lecturer, Bachelor of Nursing
School of Health Science
Massey University
New Zealand
email: S.J.Gammer@massey.ac.nz

Christine Hogg
Senior Lecturer in Mental Health Nursing
School of Nursing
The University of Salford
United Kingdom
e-mail: C.hogg@salford.ac.uk

Moira McLoughlin
Lecturer School of Nursing
Faculty of Health and Social Care
The University of Salford
United Kingdom
e-mail: M.McLoughlin@salford.ac.uk

Dr Juliana R. Mansvelt
Lecturer, School of People, Environment
    and Planning
Massey University
New Zealand
e-mail: J.R.Mansvelt@massey.ac.nz

Eula Miller
Senior Lecturer, Department of
    Healthcare Studies
Manchester Metropolitan University
United Kingdom
Email: e.miller@mmu.ac.uk

Dr Mary E. Murray
Senior Lecturer, School of Sociology,
    Social Policy and Social Work
Massey University
New Zealand
e-mail: M.Murray@massey.ac.nz

Dr Rachel Page
Director of Sport and Life Science
Institute of Food, Nutrition and Human
    Health
Massey University
New Zealand
email: R.A.Page@massey.ac.nz

Associate Professor Tim J. Parkinson
Institute of Veterinary Animal and
    Biomedical Sciences
Massey University
New Zealand
e-mail: T.J.Parkinson@massey.ac.nz

Dr Regina Pernice
Rehabilitation Co-ordinator
School of Health Sciences
Massey University
New Zealand
e-mail: R.E.Pernice@massey.ac.nz

Sophie Smailes
Lecturer, Department of Healthcare
    Studies
Manchester Metropolitan University
United Kingdom
e-mail: s.smailes@mmu.ac.uk

Dr Sheila Stark
Reader, Health Research
Department of Healthcare Studies
Manchester Metropolitan University
United Kingdom
e-mail: s.stark@mmu.ac.uk

Dr Terry M.Stewart
Senior Lecturer: Institute of Natural
    Resources
Massey University
New Zealand
e-mail: T.Stewart@massey.ac.nz

Clare Street
Senior Lecturer, Department of Health
    Care Studies
Manchester Metropolitan University
United Kingdom
e-mail: C.Street@mmu.ac.uk

Errol Thompson
Lecturer in Information Systems
Department of Information Systems
Massey University
New Zealand
e-mail: E.L.Thompson@massey.ac.nz

Kim van Wissen
Senior Lecturer, School of Health
    Sciences
Massey University
New Zealand
e-mail: K.A.VanWissen@massey.ac.nz

Katherine Watson
Lecturer, Department of Healthcare
    Studies
Manchester Metropolitan University
United Kingdom
e-mail: k.watson@mmu.ac.uk